CATHOLIC
see
SOCIAL
discern
TEACHING
act

An introduction for schools, parishes and charities

RAYMOND FRIEL

Published by **Redemptorist Publications**
Wolf's Lane, Chawton, Hampshire, GU34 3HQ, UK
Tel. +44 (0)1420 88222, Fax. +44 (0)1420 88805
Email rp@rpbooks.co.uk, www.rpbooks.co.uk

A registered charity limited by guarantee
Registered in England 03261721

First Published September 2023

Edited by Helen Birkbeck
Designed by Eliana Thompson

ISBN 978 0 85231 640 5

A CIP catalogue record for this book is available from the British Library.

Imprimatur: + Declan Lang
Bishop of Clifton
August 2023

Imprimatur is a declaration that a book or pamphlet is considered to be free from doctrinal or moral error. It is not implied that those who have granted the Imprimatur agree with the contents.

Printed by Bishops Printers,
Portsmouth, Hampshire, PO6 1TR

ACKNOWLEDGEMENTS

For fruitful conversations and messages of support and encouragement, I'd like to thank Clare Watkins, Damian Howard, David Wells, Jenny Sinclair, Jenny Heywood-Jones, Jim McManus, Liam Hayes, Lorna Gold, Maria Power, Peter Fleetwood and all the wonderful colleagues in our schools and charities who made time to talk to me and who are featured in Part II. As ever, I'd like to thank my wife, Janet, for her loving support and for the wonderful diagrams.

BY THE SAME AUTHOR

Seeing the River (Edinburgh: Polygon, 1995)

Southfields Vols 1-6, ed. with Richard Price (London: Southfields Press, 1995-2000)

Renfrewshire in Old Photographs, with Richard Price (Glasgow: Mariscat, 2000)

PS Nos 1-7, ed. with Richard Price (London: published by Richard Price, 2006-2012)

Stations of the Heart (Cambridge: Salt, 2008)

How to Survive Working in a Catholic School, with Sister Judith Russi (Chawton: Redemptorist Publications, 2013)

How to Survive in Leadership in a Catholic School (Chawton: Redemptorist Publications, 2015)

The Revolution of Tenderness: Being a Catholic in today's Church (Chawton: Redemptorist Publications, 2016)

Gospel Values for Catholic Schools: a practical guide for today (Chawton: Redemptorist Publications, 2017)

Prayers for Schools: original prayers and resources for teachers and chaplains (Chawton: Redemptorist Publications, 2018)

At Your Side: a book for those who pray, those who want to pray and those who lead prayer, with David Wells (Chawton: Redemptorist Publications, 2020)

Formation of the Heart: The Why and How of being a Catholic today (Chawton: Redemptorist Publications, 2022)

DEDICATION

To all the good people
in our schools, parishes and charities
who live out Catholic Social Teaching every day
whether they know its definitions or not.

"It is not enough merely to formulate a social doctrine. It must be translated into reality. And this is particularly true of the Church's social doctrine, the light of which is Truth, Justice its objective, and Love its driving force."

(Pope John XXIII, *Mater et Magistra*, 226)

CATHOLIC
SOCIAL
TEACHING
CATHOLIC
SOCIA
TEACHIN
CATHOLIC
SOCIAL
TEACHING
CATHOLIC

CONTENTS

INTRODUCTION

Welcome to this introduction to what is sometimes known as the Church's "best-kept secret" – Catholic Social Teaching. How did it earn such a dubious label? Perhaps it's because the documents are a bit long and full of some dense arguments and theology. Perhaps it's because it's too radical, and if we took it seriously the Church would be on a collision course with every government in the world. Take, for example, the universal destination of goods, the principle that everyone has a right to the goods of the earth, such as clean water, shelter, food. That alone would turn things upside down.

Who is this book for? Well, you, I hope, since you've been kind enough to have picked it up and read this far. It's for a lot of people I know. Good people who work in our Catholic schools, parishes and charities – whether they are Catholic or not – and who support the mission of the Church in these settings, but don't know much about Catholic Social Teaching. Our schools in particular have a fresh interest in CST now that we have a Religious Education Directory and an inspection framework (the inspection of Catholic life and RE, not Ofsted) that makes frequent reference to CST principles and its underpinning theology.

Part I tries to provide an introduction to the principles of CST, rooted in scripture and theology. Too often we just go racing to those principles and forget the scriptural and theological foundations. I've tried to keep these chapters short and have included quotations from scripture and the social encyclicals (letters) from a succession of popes. These ten chapters might form the basis of a study programme or CPD group in a school or in a parish. It won't take you long to read a chapter and at the end you'll find questions to prompt reflection and discussion. Perhaps over ten weeks, ten thirty-minute sessions could be organised to look at one chapter at a time?

Part II directs a spotlight on Catholic Social Action in some of our schools and charities. Whether people know about CST or not, the reality is that they very often embody it, they walk the talk, which is more important than knowing about a set of principles. However, knowing more about those principles and methods of approach (see Chapter Ten on See-Judge-Act) might help to shape that action in ways that are even more attuned with the Gospel. Part III is a bundle of lists and resources that I hope you will find helpful, including a CST Calendar, which picks out key dates in the year when you might want to highlight some aspect of CST or organise an event or a campaign based on the theme of the day.

I refer throughout to the *Compendium of the Social Doctrine of the Church*. This *Compendium*, published by the Vatican in 2004, is a concise and complete overview of the Church's social teaching. It is more than just a summary of all the papal encyclicals; it offers its own helpful understanding of that underpinning theology already mentioned. It is due to be revised in the light of the encyclicals that have been published since 2004, especially Pope Francis' groundbreaking encyclical *Laudato Si'*, but it is still a very helpful resource.

Catholic Social Teaching in a sense is no more than trying to view what's going on in society in our place and time through the lens of the Gospel and see what we might do to make the situation more like God's loving plan for creation. I hope that this short introduction helps you to understand this treasure of the Church a bit more and inspires you in your work of building a better world.

PART ONE

CATHOLIC SOCIAL TEACHING

Ten short reads

WHAT'S GOING ON? IS IT ALL BAD?

> ***Topics covered:*** *what's going on in society – what's happening to people – the preferential option for the poor – the inductive approach, beginning with concrete reality – God's Spirit at work in the lives of all human beings – the role of conscience – the importance of compassion* ***and*** *justice.*

"What's going on?" sang Marvin Gaye, in response to police violence against anti-war and civil rights protesters in late 1960s America. Gaye's lament could well be one of the anthems of Catholic Social Teaching (CST), which asks the same question: *what's going on?* CST begins with reality, the situation here and now. Specifically, CST asks the question: *what's happening to people, especially those who are poor?* What are the relationships like between people in this place? Where are people flourishing and where are they held back and diminished by poverty or injustice? What can be done to make this situation more in conformity with God's vision of justice and peace for the whole human race?

Catholic theology didn't always start with the here and now. It was more likely to start with the divine and work down to the human (known as the *deductive* method). The change in this approach is a feature of Catholic Social Teaching, as we can see, for example, in *Gaudium et Spes*, a key document of Vatican II (the gathering of all the world's bishops for a Council in Rome over four sessions from 1962 to 1965). One of the last documents they approved, *Gaudium et Spes* (The Pastoral Constitution on the Church in the Modern World), is arguably the most authoritative Church document on Catholic Social Teaching, so it's a document worthy of your study. Its first sentence is memorable:

> The joys and hopes and the sorrows and anxieties of people today, especially of those who are poor and afflicted, are also the joys and hopes, sorrows and anxieties of the disciples of Christ, and there is nothing truly human which does not also affect them.[1]

It starts with the human scene, the joys and sorrows of *everybody*, not just religious people. This turning to the modern world in love and friendship was a key feature of Vatican II. Previously, the Church had been defensive and suspicious of modernity and progress. New ideologies in the nineteenth century talked about the human person and society with no reference to God. The Church doubled down in opposition to all this, appearing to be socially conservative, aloof, judgemental. That all changed at the Council. The starting point was concern for what was happening to people, at the grassroots, from the bottom up (an *inductive* method). The Church stood in **solidarity** with humankind, saying your joys and sorrows are ours too.

One important point to note from that first sentence in *Gaudium et Spes* is the emphasis on those who are poor. Inspired by Jesus in the Gospels, whose mission was to proclaim good news to the poor and liberty to the oppressed (Luke 4:18), the Church has a **preferential option for the poor**, because God opts for the poor. The *Catechism of the Catholic Church* says that "those who are oppressed by poverty are the object of a preferential love on the part of the Church which, since her origin and in spite of the failings of many of her members, has not ceased to work for their relief, defence and liberation".[2] What that looks like in practice today is a challenge to which Pope Francis has drawn our attention time and time again. What does a poor Church for the poor look like?

In the early days of the Christian community, property and possessions were shared and money was collected to relieve the suffering of the destitute (Acts 4:32; Galatians 2:10; 1 Corinthians 16:1-4). This attention to the most vulnerable was also a feature of the Jewish faith from which Christianity sprang, so it's no surprise that this should have happened. The emphasis, however, was often on compassion, on the relief of poverty, not on challenging its causes. It is only in recent times that we've seen an emphasis on compassion *and* justice. Help the poor *and* ask the question, *what's going on to make people poor?* **Justice** is not an abstract idea, but something you *do*, a habit, a virtue, a commitment to ensuring that people receive what they are due in order to lead fully human lives. This is also known as social justice. For the other types of justice, see paragraph 2411 of the *Catechism of the Catholic Church*.

The Church's social teaching invites us to "read" society, the signs of the times, to see what's really going on, and then decide what we can do to make the situation better for people, especially those who are poor. The purpose of this habitual work (it is in fact another virtue, but we'll come back to that later) is not to judge the world but to serve the world, to try to "build a better world based upon truth and justice".[3] God is on our side in this project. In fact, he's on the *in*side of the project. The teaching of the Council is that God is at work in the world, in every human heart that is receptive, gently prompting us towards the good. Humanity is being "stirred by the Spirit of God".[4] The Gospel is described as a ferment or yeast that stimulates in the human heart "the irresistible demands of dignity".[5] We have an instinct for **dignity**, for what it means to be fully human. This "instinct" is our conscience, the inner place, our heart, where God speaks to us, prompting us to do good and avoid what is harmful.

It's not easy to look at the world the way Jesus did. It's the work of a lifetime, but CST invites us to embark on that journey. Our perceptions of people and situations are shaped by how we were brought up, the values we inherited or adopted, the part of the world we live in, our ethnicity, our class, our gender, our life experience. CST is about rebooting our perceptual apparatus, in order to see things differently. Pope Benedict XVI put it this way: "The Christian's programme – the programme of the Good Samaritan, the programme of Jesus – is 'a heart which sees'. This heart sees where love is needed and acts accordingly."[6]

In other words, we're invited to see what's going on with the loving eyes of Jesus. Love is the beating heart of the Gospel and it's the foundation of Catholic Social Teaching. Love is the wellspring of the fundamental Gospel values of truth, freedom and justice. Love is what animates and inspires justice. Love is more than a feeling. It is, like justice, something you do, a habit, another virtue, but the highest of the virtues, a constant disposition towards the good of the other, with no expectation of affirming feedback, no hint of exploitation or coercion. Love is presence, encounter, accompaniment. Love is having skin in the game. It is a journey out of ourselves and our own narrow interests. It is the highest vocation of the human being, since we cannot find fulfilment in ourselves, but only "*with* and *for* others".[7] Love is, as St Paul said, "patient and kind" (1 Cor. 13:4). Love tempers justice. Love wants to make a difference:

> It is undoubtedly an act of love, the work of mercy by which one responds here and now to a real and impelling need of one's neighbour, but it is an equally indispensable act of love to strive to organise and structure society so that one's neighbour will not find himself in poverty.[8]

This is why, as Pope Francis says, Catholic Social Teaching is primarily positive, since it "offers proposals, it works for change and in this sense it constantly points to the hope born of the loving heart of Jesus Christ".[9] We don't start with condemnation of the world; we start with what is good, the events and developments where the Spirit is at work, especially at a local level, and seek to bring them to fruition. This does not mean we are blind to the negative. CST also offers a critique of the trends in society that are harmful, the barriers to the common good. CST denounces injustice, as well as proclaiming good news. In *Laudato Si'* (2015) and *Fratelli Tutti* (2020), Pope Francis is very clear about the interlinked dangers of consumerist individualism and a throwaway culture, a virus which leads to injustice, indifference to the needs of others and environmental destruction. In St Luke's account of the Beatitudes, we hear Jesus declaring "woes" (to the rich and powerful) as well as "blessings" (to the poor) (Luke 6:20-26).

Human beings are good, but flawed, in some cases very flawed, but God works in human hearts, prompting us all the time towards the good. What holds us back is what the Christian tradition calls **original sin**, which we'll look at more closely in Chapter Three. CST is not utopian. We don't anticipate heaven on earth, although a utopian vision can be inspiring. We know that for every outbreak of grace – the effervescent life of God – in a human heart, or in a household, or in a community, there will be a hardening of hearts, a resistance to grace. In this life, we don't anticipate an end to injustice or suffering, a return to the Garden of Eden, but we can try to limit the effects of injustice and reduce suffering; and where we can, build up God's kingdom of love and justice.

Over the next few chapters, we'll look at the main principles of Catholic Social Teaching, rooted in scripture and the teaching of the Church. After the principles, we'll look at some examples of Catholic Social Action. The Gospel always calls us to action for good in the world. The role of CST is to help us to see what needs to be done and how best to do it. It's a Gospel way of looking at the world. Let's put our new glasses on.

Questions for individual reflection or group discussion:
Where is the "good news" of compassion and justice in your own community? What is happening that looks like the work of the Holy Spirit breaking through? It could be a community coming together to help and befriend the vulnerable and isolated, a new scheme of sharing and gift exchange, a credit union to help people avoid crippling interest payments, a food pantry to feed the hungry with dignity, a campaign to improve the wages or conditions of local workers, new ways to reduce the carbon footprint and live simply and sustainably. How might you support those efforts?

Quotations from sacred scripture and the teaching of the Church:

"The Pharisees and Sadducees came, and to test Jesus they asked him to show them a sign from heaven. He answered them, 'When it is evening, you say, "It will be fair weather, for the sky is red." And in the morning, "It will be stormy today, for the sky is red and threatening." You know how to interpret the appearance of the sky, but you cannot interpret the signs of the times.'"

Matthew 16:1-3

"Deep within their conscience individuals discover a law which they do not make for themselves but which they are bound to obey, whose voice, ever summoning them to love and do what is good and to avoid what is evil, rings in their hearts when necessary with the command: Do this, keep away from that. For inscribed in their hearts by God, human beings have a law whose observance is their dignity and in accordance with which they are to be judged. Conscience is the most intimate centre and sanctuary of a person, in which he or she is alone with God whose voice echoes within them."

Gaudium et Spes[10]

"To believe that the Holy Spirit is at work in everyone means realizing that he seeks to penetrate every human situation and all social bonds: The Holy Spirit can be said to possess an infinite creativity, proper to the divine mind, which knows how to loosen the knots of human affairs, even the most complex and inscrutable."

Pope Francis[11]

"God continues to sow abundant seeds of goodness in our human family."

Pope Francis[12]

"Mother and Teacher, the Church does not close herself off nor retreat within herself but is always open, reaching out to and turned towards man, whose destiny of salvation is her reason for being. She is in the midst of men and women as the living icon of the Good Shepherd, who goes in search of and finds man where he is, in the existential and historical circumstances of his life. It is there that the Church becomes for man a point of contact with the Gospel, with the message of liberation and reconciliation, of justice and peace."

Compendium of the Social Doctrine of the Church[13]

"The school is an institution where young people gradually learn to open themselves up to life as it is, and to create in themselves a definite attitude to life as it should be."

The Catholic School[14]

References

1. Second Vatican Council, *Gaudium et Spes* (Pastoral Constitution on the Church in the Modern World), 1.
2. *Catechism of the Catholic Church*, 2448.
3. Second Vatican Council, *Gaudium et Spes* (Pastoral Constitution on the Church in the Modern World), 55.
4. Second Vatican Council, *Gaudium et Spes* (Pastoral Constitution on the Church in the Modern World), 41.
5. Second Vatican Council, *Gaudium et Spes* (Pastoral Constitution on the Church in the Modern World), 26.
6. Pope Benedict XVI, *Deus Caritas Est* ("On Christian Love"), 31.
7. *Compendium of the Social Doctrine of the Church* (London: Bloomsbury, 2004), 165.
8. *Compendium,* 208.
9. Pope Francis, *Evangelii Gaudium* ("The Joy of the Gospel"), 183.
10. *Gaudium et Spes*, 16.
11. Pope Francis, *Evangelii Gaudium*, 178.
12. Pope Francis, *Fratelli Tutti*, 54.
13. *Compendium*, 86.
14. The Congregation for Catholic Education, *The Catholic School*, 31.

IN THE BEGINNING: THE FOUNDATIONS

> ***Topics covered:*** *key themes in Genesis chapter 1 that are foundational to Catholic Social Teaching – creation as the gift of God – creation as good – men and women as made in the image of God – human beings as co-creators with God – created goods intended for the sustenance of all – concept of one human family – sabbath rest.*

The year 1891 is regarded by many as the year Catholic Social Teaching began. This makes good sense, since it was the year that Pope Leo XIII published his encyclical *Rerum Novarum* (encyclicals are named after the first phrase in the Latin version of the text, in this case, "Of new things"), the first papal letter in modern times to address the question of *what's going on* in society, in particular the plight of workers in the industrialised age. This is the *magna carta* of Catholic Social Teaching. It is a remarkable document in many ways, and we'll come back to it later on. However, I'd like to start our exploration of the principles of CST earlier than 1891. I'd like to start at the very beginning.

Genesis, the first book of the Bible, begins with the phrase: "In the beginning when God created the heavens and the earth…" (Genesis 1:1). This account of creation was probably written by a group of Jewish priests in exile in Babylon sometime around the middle of the sixth century BC. Their capital city, Jerusalem, had been destroyed by the mighty Babylonian army. Their Temple, the heart of their religious practice, the place where God himself dwelled (*shekinah*), had been levelled in a frenzy of destruction. They were deported to Babylon, around 800 miles away, where they sat down and wept.

In the culture of their oppressors, they would have come across stories about the beginning of the world (*creation myths*) in which all things came to be as a result of violent conflict between the gods. In these accounts, human beings were usually described as slaves at the service of the gods who were quite keen on a life of heavenly indolence. Despite the trauma of their uprooting from Jerusalem, the Jewish priests wrote their own account of creation, which was quite different from the Babylonian version. There was no cosmic carnage, no enslaved humankind, just a gracious moment of creating when the Spirit of God (in Hebrew, *ruach*) swept over the waters of chaos (*tohu wa bohu*) and God said, "Let there be light" (1:3). And there was light.

If you're not familiar with this passage of the Bible, or haven't read it for a while, I'd suggest you take a few minutes to read over it again, from the beginning of chapter 1 up to chapter 2, verse 3. This is the account of the creation of the heavens and the earth, the plants, the trees, the creatures and, finally, human beings, male and female. They are not named in this story; that comes in the next chapter, which is another account of creation, the one with the Garden of Eden, Adam and Eve, the serpent and the fruit. That's the story that deals with how sin came into the world. In chapter 1, however, there is no mention of sin. It's just a glorious hymn about how God created the good earth and all its inhabitants.

From a Catholic Social Teaching point of view, so many of the foundational principles can be found in this passage of scripture. Here are some of the main insights taken from the teaching of the Church:

God is the Creator. God is not a part of creation. We are not God; we are created, part of creation. Nor can God be said to *be* creation – that's known as *pantheism*. God is, however, close to creation. The Church teaches that God is "present to his creatures' inmost being".[1] In the words of St Augustine, God is "higher than my highest and more inward than my innermost being".[2] As we noted in Chapter One, God is lovingly present to and active in his creatures.

God creates "out of nothing". Creation is not some kind of emanation from the divine substance, or the reshaping of material that was already in existence. The *Catechism* points out that a human artist creates from a given material, "while God shows his power by starting from nothing to make all he wants".[3]

Creation is the gift of God. It is gratuitous. This is the underlying reality of our existence: gift and gratuity (not entitlement). Any gift, when received *as* a gift, calls us to a response of gratitude. One of the great lies of the modern age is that creation, including human beings, is a commodity, to be bought and sold, plundered and extracted, not a gift to be cherished. Our conscience also senses that we are called "to manage responsibly and together with others the gift received".[4] We can see proof of this in the universal recognition of the golden rule: "In everything do to others as you would have them do to you" (Matthew 7:12). The *Catechism* tells us that "God has no other reason for creating than his love and goodness".[5]

Creation is good. Some schools of thought over the centuries have considered the physical world to be evil and sinful (for example, Gnosticism). Nothing evil comes from God. Five times in the first chapter of Genesis, God says that what he has made is "good". On the sixth day, he declares all he has made, including human beings, to be "very good" (1:31). Imagine God writing that on the palm of your hand, like an artist's comment: *very good*. Creation bears witness to God, the divine artist.

Men and women are made in the image and likeness of God (1:27)**.** Being made in the image of God is what bestows on the human being their fundamental dignity. This is the foundational principle of Catholic Social Teaching. We are not a something, but a some*one*. In the teaching of the Church, this means we are capable of "self-knowledge, of self-possession and of freely giving [ourselves] and entering into communion with other persons".[6]

In other words, the vocation of the human person is to love and be loved, to be self-aware and to make free choices. We are fundamentally relational beings and can attain our full identity "only in sincere self-giving".[7]

Men and women are co-creators with God. This is another aspect of our dignity, "for God grants his creatures not only their existence, but also the dignity of acting on their own, of being causes and principles for each other, and this co-operating in the accomplishment of his plan".[8] We are given "dominion" (1:26) over creation, but in the way that images of God might have dominion; that is, to be cultivators and custodians of creation, not to exploit, abuse or destroy creation. Men and women are called to "be fruitful and multiply" (1:28), to procreate; in other words to create on God's behalf.

Creation is abundant and for all. God gave us the plants and "every tree with seed in its fruit" (1:29) for food. It is interesting that this is a vegetarian diet; there is no mention of eating the creatures. There is nothing parsimonious about this gift of food. There is an abundance of food and plenty to go round. In Catholic Social Teaching this becomes the key concept of **the universal destination of goods**, which is summed up in *Gaudium et Spes* as follows: "God has destined the earth and all it contains for the use of everyone and of all peoples, so that the good things of creation should be available equally to all, with justice to guide and charity in attendance."[9] People have a *right* to that part of the goods of the earth they need to sustain and develop life.

Men and women have a common origin. Because of our common origin in God, "the human race forms a unity".[10] We are all made equal in dignity as human beings by God. No person, or race, or country is inferior to any other. Our common origin is the source of human solidarity and love. We are all, in our wonderful diversity, truly brothers and sisters. During the lockdowns in the

COVID pandemic, we saw this sense of unity, of fraternity, rise to the surface. We looked out for one another. We were thankful to the people who kept us alive. As the pandemic ebbed away, so did the sense of fraternity, to a large extent. But we know it's there; it still breaks through, just not on such a movingly massive scale. Pope Francis encourages us not to let the dream die: "Let us dream, then, as a single human family, as fellow travellers sharing the same flesh, as children of the same earth which is our common home, each of us bringing the richness of his or her beliefs and convictions, each of us with his or her own voice, brothers and sisters all."[11]

The seventh day is a day of rest. On the seventh day, when God had completed the work of creation, he rested (2:2). He blessed the seventh day, the sabbath, and made it holy. This in the great tradition of the Jewish people was when no work was to be done, even by the livestock, and all attention was to be on the word of God and worship of God. Work is not everything. Rest restores the three fundamental relationships at the heart of the biblical vision of being truly human. Pope Francis explains it like this:

> The creation accounts in the book of Genesis contain, in their own symbolic and narrative language, profound teachings about human existence and its historical reality. They suggest that human life is grounded in three fundamental and closely intertwined relationships: with God, with our neighbour and with the earth itself.[12]

In the second account of creation, with Adam and Eve, the serpent and the fruit, we hear the story of how this life-giving circuit of relationships is broken, the mandate of dominion is corrupted and human society is consumed by violence. We'll look at that more closely in the next chapter, but for now let's reflect on how much richness was contained in those few verses in Genesis written by people who were far from home and all they held dear. In their exile, they experienced a remarkable deepening of faith. They encountered a God who made the world out of love and bestowed upon his human creatures a dignity and a vocation to love and be partners in the great project of creation.

Questions for individual reflection or group discussion:

Of the key themes identified in the first chapter of Genesis as foundational to Catholic Social Teaching, do any surprise you, or challenge you? Do you find this scriptural approach helpful?

Quotations from sacred scripture and the teaching of the Church:

> "For you love all things that exist, and detest none of the things that you have made; for you would not have made anything if you had hated it. How would anything have endured if you had not willed it? Or how would anything not called forth by you have been preserved? You spare all things, for they are yours, O LORD, you who love the living."
>
> Wisdom 11:24-26

> "Created in God's image, we were given the mandate to transform the earth. By their work people share in God's creating activity... Awareness that our work is a sharing in God's work ought to permeate even the most ordinary daily activities. By our labour we are unfolding the Creator's work and contributing to the realization of God's plan on earth. The Christian message does not stop us from building the world or make us neglect our fellow human beings. On the contrary it binds us more firmly to do just that."
>
> Pope John Paul II[13]

"In today's world, the sense of belonging to a single human family is fading, and the dream of working together for justice and peace seems an outdated utopia. What reigns instead is a cool, comfortable and globalized indifference, born of deep disillusionment concealed behind a deceptive illusion: thinking that we are all-powerful, while failing to realize that we are all in the same boat. This illusion, unmindful of the great fraternal values, leads to a sort of cynicism. For that is the temptation we face if we go down the road of disenchantment and disappointment... Isolation and withdrawal into one's own interests are never the way to restore hope and bring about renewal. Rather, it is closeness; it is the culture of encounter."

Pope Francis[14]

References

1. *Catechism of the Catholic Church*, 300.
2. *Catechism*, 300.
3. *Catechism*, 296.
4. *Compendium of the Social Doctrine of the Church* (London: Bloomsbury, 2004), 20.
5. *Catechism*, 293.
6. *Catechism*, 357.
7. Second Vatican Council, *Gaudium et Spes* (Pastoral Constitution on the Church in the Modern World), 24.
8. *Catechism*, 306.
9. *Gaudium et Spes*, 69.
10. *Catechism*, 360.
11. Pope Francis, *Fratelli Tutti* ("On Fraternity and Social Friendship"), 8.
12. Pope Francis, *Laudato Si'* ("On Care for Our Common Home"), 66.
13. Pope John Paul II, *Laborem Exercens*, 25.
14. *Fratelli Tutti*, 30.

ORIGINAL SIN AND THE PROPHETIC CALL FOR JUSTICE

> ***Topics covered:*** *the second account of creation – the dignity of the person and the right to life – covenant and care for the earth – the fall from grace – original sin – the understanding of poverty in the Old Testament and the preferential option for those who are vulnerable – the prophets for social justice.*

In the second chapter of the book of Genesis we find another account of creation. This should not lead us to ask, *well, which one is true, then?* They are both figurative accounts, inspired stories if you like, which convey a fundamental truth: God made the world and human beings out of love. The second account of creation is, literally, more earthy. God "formed" (2:7) man (in Hebrew, *adam*) from the "dust of the soil" (*adamah*). The Hebrew wordplay speaks of the intimate closeness of human beings and the earth. We are of the same stuff.

The first Genesis version of the creation of human beings is more like liturgy than story, a kind of hymn to creation. God said let us make humankind in our image and then he makes humankind in his image. But there's no description of the process, or the product, the human beings. We know they are good, but we don't see or hear them. In the second account, God "formed" (2:7) the man. It's the same word that is used for a potter forming or shaping clay. We have our origin and purpose in the creative loving intention and design of God. We are not here by some random coming together of circumstances in the universe. God "breathed into his nostrils the breath of life; and the man became a living being" (2:7). There is an intimacy and physicality in this account: we are made alive by the very breath of God in us.

The earthiness of this creation story is the origin of our belief in the bond between the human being, the earth and God. There is no reference here to the phrase "image and likeness of God" from chapter 1 that is so essential to our understanding of human dignity. The same point, however, is made even more powerfully by the fact that we are animated by the very breath of God. This is our dignity. This is why the Church so firmly believes in the sanctity of life, from conception to natural death. This is why the first "right" in Catholic Social Teaching is the right to life. Not all rights are equal. The right to life is first and foremost. To take a life, or to degrade or exploit a life, is a grave injustice, a breach in the right order of things.

Having breathed life into Adam, God decided that he should not be alone but should have a partner. While Adam was asleep, God took one of his ribs and fashioned Eve, the first woman. They were made for each other. If the first covenant (an enduring loving relationship) in the Bible is between God and creation, then the second is between Adam and Eve. They became "one flesh" (2:24). It's important to note here that the Church teaches that men and women are equal. The *Catechism* tells us that "Man and woman have been created, which is to say, willed by God: on the one hand, in perfect equality as human persons; on the other, in their respective beings as man and woman".[1] They are equal in dignity.

Men and women, then, were intended to live in a state of holiness (closeness to God) and justice (in right relationship, in harmony with God, each other and creation, receiving what was "due" to them to live as human beings). In Genesis 2, they were put in the garden of the world to "till it and keep it" (2:15). This is an even clearer commission than Genesis 1. Our role is to cultivate the earth for the common good. This was the original plan of God. For humans to be relational, fruitful and creative, to be co-creators in the great project of life. But, as creatures, we have limits. We are not God. The tree in the garden with its "forbidden fruit" – the fruit God says we should not eat – is a symbol of the limits involved in being subject to the laws of creation.

Enter the serpent. The Bible doesn't specify here that the serpent is the devil, but, as Pope Benedict XVI said, is better understood as a symbol of "that wisdom which rules the world".[2] At the heart of the story of eating the forbidden fruit is a profound truth about human beings: we didn't trust the original plan of God for us, that plan of holiness and justice. We reached out for more; we disobeyed. This is what we understand by sin, in this case original sin, the sin of a "fallen" human race, inclined to grasp what we should not. Pope Francis gives us a memorable definition:

> Our sin lies in failing to recognise value, in wanting to possess and exploit that which we do not value as gift. Sin always has this same root of possessiveness, of enrichment at the expense of other people and creation itself... The sin is in exploiting what must not be exploited, in extracting wealth (power or satisfaction) from where it should not be taken. Sin is a rejection of the limits that love requires.[3]

Original sin – the "sin of the world" (John 1:29) – is what we're born into. We are inclined to sin, what the teaching of the Church calls concupiscence. We get it wrong, we can be selfish, we look for happiness in the wrong places, we try to dominate and exploit other people. This does not change that original vision of us as very good, or the fact that the Holy Spirit is still at work in us. Nor does it take away our responsibility for what we do. Our actions are not determined (generally speaking); we are free to make choices. The more we are open to the grace of God, the better those choices will be. We are a mixed blessing. We are very good, but flawed, with an inclination to do things that are not very good. Notice in Genesis 3:16 that one of the consequences of sin is a breach in the equality of the relationship between Adam and Eve. God says to Eve that Adam "will rule over you". This is a distortion of the right relations between them. We also see that their relationship with the earth is corrupted. As the human race expands, we see the spread of violence (Genesis 6:5-7), with one person, one group, one nation, trying to dominate another by force. Injustice has come into the land. And with injustice come exploitation and poverty. The blues have entered the human story.

Throughout the Old Testament, we see the consequences of original sin, expressed in personal sin and social sin. In the history of Israel, in the history of every society, there is poverty. An important point to underscore in Catholic Social Teaching is that material poverty – the deprivation that prevents people from living fully human lives – is not willed by God. The cause of poverty, this scandalous condition, is the injustice of oppressors, the behaviour of wicked people. There are many descriptions of this in scripture; one of the most memorable is in the book of Job:

> The wicked remove landmarks;
> they seize flocks and pasture them.
> They drive away the donkey of the orphan;
> they take the widow's ox for a pledge.
> They thrust the needy off the road;
> the poor of the earth all hide themselves.
> Like wild asses in the desert
> they go out to their toil,
> scavenging in the waste-land
> food for their young.
> They reap in a field not their own
> and they glean in the vineyard of the wicked.
> They lie all night naked, without clothing,
> and have no covering in the cold.
> They are wet with the rain of the mountains,
> and cling to the rock for want of shelter,
>
> Job 24:2-8

In this vivid account of destitution (which is the most acute form of poverty – not having enough to sustain existence), it is clear that the human beings who are in such a pitiable state are there because of the unjust and violent actions of wicked people, their oppressors. Their poverty is not some kind of destiny, or, as some would still say today, the result of laziness or lack of initiative. It is the result of injustice, with roots in original sin. They do not have what is due to them, their share of the earth's resources to sustain a flourishing life. In his despair, Job thinks that "God pays no attention to their prayer" (24:12), but the Bible attests throughout that God is moved by the suffering of the afflicted. God is on the side of those who are poor; to know God is to work for justice for those who are poor and oppressed.

When the Israelites were slaves in Egypt, God was moved by their situation. He tells Moses, in whom he had stirred a vocation to be their liberator, that "I have observed the misery of my people… I have come down to deliver them from the Egyptians" (Exodus 3:7-8). God will work through the (reluctant) human agency of Moses to liberate his people from slavery and exploitation. When they are in the wilderness on their long journey to the Promised Land, God gives them laws to help them live as human beings. The Ten Commandments that God issued on Mount Sinai are all about just relationships with God, with each other, with creation. In the more detailed laws that follow in the book of Exodus, God shows his commitment to the resident aliens, the widows and the orphans (the most vulnerable members of the community):

> You shall not wrong or oppress a resident alien, for you were aliens in the land of Egypt. You shall not abuse any widow or orphan. If you do abuse them, when they cry out to me, I will surely heed their cry… And if your neighbour cries out to me, I will listen, for I am compassionate.
>
> Exodus 22:21-27

Since we are inclined to ignore even what God says, these laws were frequently broken and vulnerable people were abused and exploited. God did not just sit in heaven shaking his head in dismay at this behaviour. He stirred a vocation in some to be prophets to denounce injustice, and announce a better way to live. The Old Testament prophets didn't hold back when it came to speaking truth to power. The role of a prophet was not to predict the future, but to speak on God's behalf. They showed up *what was going on*, they called it out, they told it as it was and as it should be. Injustice is not part of God's plan. The prophet Isaiah spoke out against those "who make iniquitous decrees, who write oppressive statutes, to turn aside the needy from justice and to rob the poor of my people of their right, that widows may be your spoil, and that you may make orphans your prey!" (Isaiah 10:1-2). The prophet Micah neatly summed up what God expects of us, which is "to do justice, and to love kindness, and to walk humbly with your God" (Micah 6:8).

To oppress the poor is to offend the image of God in the human person. It is contrary to the will of God, who wants human beings to live in peace and justice, in a beloved community of human flourishing. But there can be no peace without justice. Isaiah says that "the effect of righteousness [justice] will be peace, and the result of righteousness, quietness and trust for ever" (32:17). Even right at the beginning of the story of sin, when Adam and Eve had eaten the forbidden fruit, God came looking for them. "Where are you?" (Genesis 3:9), God calls out to Adam and Eve, who are hiding, ashamed of their lack of trust in their Creator. The story of the Bible in many ways is the story of God's search for his lost creatures, to free them from injustice. This search comes to its wonderful climax when God, in Jesus, becomes a human being to redeem us from the "sin of the world" that has led to so much suffering, so much injustice, so many heartfelt cries of woe.

Questions for individual reflection or group discussion:

Does this view of sin surprise you? What is your own understanding of sin? Does this description of the Old Testament surprise or challenge you? What was your own image of the Old Testament? Can you begin to express what a "preferential option for the poor" might look like in your setting?

Quotations from sacred scripture and the teaching of the Church:

"If there is among you anyone in need, a member of your community in any of your towns within the land that the LORD your God is giving you, do not be hard-hearted or tight-fisted towards your needy neighbour. You should rather open your hand, willingly lending enough to meet the need, whatever it may be."

Deuteronomy 15:7-8

"Blessed are you who are poor, for yours is the kingdom of God. Blessed are you who are hungry now, for you will be filled. Blessed are you who weep now, for you will laugh...

But woe to you who are rich, for you have received your consolation. Woe to you who are full now, for you will be hungry. Woe to you who are laughing now, for you will mourn and weep."

Luke 6:20-25

"Every method of education founded, wholly or in part, on the denial or forgetfulness of original sin and of grace, and relying on the sole powers of human nature, is unsound."

Pope Pius XI[4]

> "In its various forms – material deprivation, unjust oppression, physical and psychological illness and death – human misery is the obvious sign of the inherited condition of frailty and need for salvation in which man finds himself as a consequence of original sin. This misery elicited the compassion of Christ the Saviour, who willingly took it upon himself and identified himself with the least of his brethren."
>
> *Catechism of the Catholic Church*[5]

> "The harmony in which they found themselves, thanks to original justice, is now destroyed: the control of the soul's spiritual faculties over the body is shattered; the union of the man and woman becomes subject to tensions, their relations henceforth marked by lust and domination."
>
> *Catechism of the Catholic Church*[6]

References

1. *Catechism of the Catholic Church*, 369.
2. Pope Benedict XVI, *In the Beginning: a Catholic understanding of creation and the fall* (London: T&T Clark, 1995), 66.
3. Pope Francis, *Let Us Dream: the path to a better future* (London: Simon & Schuster, 2020), 34.
4. Pope Pius XI, *Divini Illius Magistri*, 60.
5. *Catechism of the Catholic Church*, 2448.
6. *Catechism of the Catholic Church*, 400.

JESUS THE REDEEMER: LET THE OPPRESSED GO FREE

> ***Topics covered:*** *the Incarnation – liberation of the oppressed – preferential option for the poor – integral salvation – the reign of God – divestment of power and possessions – idolatry of wealth – the transformation of relationships – the sharing of possessions.*

The good news, as we discussed in the previous chapter, is that God is not on the side of the oppressors, the human beings and the systems they create to exploit other human beings for their own profit or pleasure. God is on the side of those who are poor and oppressed. This theme runs strongly through the Bible, from the liberation of the people of Israel from slavery in Egypt to the birth of Jesus of Nazareth, the Word of God made flesh, in poverty. If God had a natural affinity with worldly power and prestige, then you might expect his human life to begin in a gilded cot in a palace. As we know from Midnight Mass and our Christmas plays in school, Jesus was born in a manger – a kind of trough where they fed the animals in the poor homes of the Middle East – in a small town on the edge of the Roman Empire. He was born on the margins, not at the centre. He was born in poverty: God's solidarity for ever with the human race, especially those who are poor.

In St Luke's Gospel, when Mary, the mother of Jesus, is newly pregnant, she visits her elderly cousin Elizabeth, who is also pregnant by a miracle of God. The two women greet each other with joy. The song that Mary sings introduces the main theme of the Gospel: a new vision for humanity, a reversal of human expectations, the hungry filled with good things, the rich sent away empty (Luke 1:46-56). In the Catholic Church we often have an image of Mary as a passive, pious, Western-looking young woman with eyes raised to heaven. The image in Luke's Gospel is more like that of a prophet of social justice: "He has brought down the powerful from their thrones, and lifted up the lowly" (Luke 1:52).

This is a political vision, a vision of a transformed humanity where justice reigns. Mary is speaking in the Old Testament prophetic tradition.

The first people outside his family to hear the good news of the birth of Jesus are the shepherds in the fields, people of low social rank. The angel appears to them and announces the good news that a saviour has been born, a messiah, the anointed one of God. They go to Bethlehem and find Mary and Joseph, and the child lying in the manger, just as the angel said. The shepherds, representatives of all those who are poor in human history, are the first to visit the saviour. After eight days, the child is circumcised, according to Jewish Law. They named him Jesus, as the angel said they should when he visited Mary to announce her conception by the Holy Spirit (Luke 1:31). The name Jesus means *God saves*. But what does God save us from? Let us look at that now, through the lens of the public ministry of Jesus, which is introduced by John the Baptist.

In Luke's Gospel, we have the most extensive account of the preaching of John the Baptist, an ascetic figure who ministered in the Judean wilderness, far from the centres of religious and political power. He urged the people who came to him in their thousands to repent, to change their minds and hearts and be forgiven for their sins. This was not just some private spiritual affair. At the heart of this conversion is the use of possessions, in other words your *lifestyle*, a major theme in Luke's Gospel. The crowds came to him and said, "What then should we do?" (Luke 3:10). He replied that if you have two coats, give one to the person who has no coat; share your food with those who have none; if you're a tax collector, don't exploit people for your own gain; if you're a soldier, don't use your power to extort money from people. The prophet's programme is about how you use your position in life and material possessions in a just way: giving alms, helping those who are without, not exploiting or adding to injustice.

When Jesus is baptised by John on the banks of the River Jordan, he is confirmed in his identity. The heavens open, the Holy Spirit descends on him in the form of a dove, and a voice says, "You are my Son, the Beloved" (Luke 3:22). After his baptism, Jesus is led by the Holy Spirit into the wilderness, where he is tempted for forty days. In the course of his temptations, he discerns what his mission is *not*. One of the temptations is to use power and authority as it is used in "the kingdoms of the world" (Luke 4:5), which the devil shows Jesus in all their glittering seduction. Jesus rejects this type of power. He is not going to be that kind of leader. This is reinforced at the end of the Gospel, at the Last Supper, when the disciples are arguing about who is the greatest. They are still in the old world of rivalry and competition. Jesus tells them that the world's leadership model is about lording it over others. Then comes the moment of revolution in human history: "But not so with you" (Luke 22:26). Leaders who follow Jesus should serve, since Jesus came among us "as one who serves" (Luke 22:27). The reversal of expectations includes an inversion of power. No more lording it over others, no more exploitation, no more injustice. Jesus calls his disciples to a *divestment* of power and possessions, to service of others, especially the needy.

After the temptation in the wilderness, Jesus returns to his home town of Nazareth and, in a moment of great drama, stands up in the synagogue, unrolls the scroll of the prophet Isaiah, and announces his mission. This is sometimes known as the Nazareth Manifesto, the most extended treatment in the Gospels of the inauguration of the public ministry of Jesus. The first thing that God, in Jesus, says about his mission on earth is that he has come to bring "good news to the poor" (Luke 4:18). Again, the poor are the priority. He continues, editing Isaiah as he goes to make the point even clearer: his mission is about release for captives, recovery of sight for the blind, freedom for the oppressed, a year of the Lord's favour. The mission of Jesus is characterised by the proclamation of the truth of God, the restoration of just relations and, above all, compassion, especially for those who are excluded or suffering. His own townspeople are enraged by this and want to lynch him. Why? Part of their expectation of the messiah was to bring vengeance on their enemies, but there is no violence in the mission of Jesus. True prophets are rejected because they challenge violence and injustice.

The year of the Lord's favour is a reference to the Old Testament law of the sabbatical year (celebrated every seven years) and the jubilee year (celebrated every fifty years). These laws – whether they were ever carried out or not – provide a vision of a resetting and rebalancing of society. The legislation says that, in these years, fields should lie fallow for the poor to use, debts should be cancelled and slaves should be allowed to return to their homes (Exodus 23; Leviticus 25; Deuteronomy 15). These principles, as it says in the *Compendium*, are "invoked in order to transform, continuously and from within, the life of the people of the Covenant, so that this life will correspond to God's plan".[1] And God's plan is for human flourishing, not for humans to be trapped in poverty, debt or slavery. It is a vision that deals with economic poverty and social injustice; a vision that sides with the oppressed against the creditors and the owners: two categories of people that in our society are given a disproportionate amount of power.

Jesus has come to save us, to liberate us from all that oppresses human beings and excludes us from participation in community, all the relationships and attachments that tie us down and prevent us from living the fully human lives God intended for us. It is not just a spiritual liberation, not just liberation from sin; or, rather, it is liberation from sin *and* all its social consequences. In Catholic Social Teaching this is known as **integral salvation**. It concerns the human person in all their dimensions: personal and social, spiritual and physical. We find this in Luke's Gospel. When Jesus cures the lepers, the Greek word *sesoken* has been translated as "your faith has *saved you*" and "your faith has *made you well*" (Luke 17:19). At the root of the word is the idea of being rescued, brought to safety.

When Jesus saved/made well the Gerasene Demoniac, who lived among the tombs in a waking nightmare of exclusion, psychosis and self-harm, Jesus said to him, "Return to your home, and declare how much God has done for you" (Luke 8:39). We see the same strategy of inclusion in Jesus' practice of unconditional table fellowship as a way of inviting the marginal and stigmatised into the friendship of God. In the parable of the Great Dinner, we hear about the host whose guests had refused his invitation since they were too busy with the concerns of the world. So he tells his servant to "go out at once into the streets and lanes of the town and bring in the poor, the crippled, the blind, and the lame" (Luke 14:21). An important dimension of salvation is about restoring the excluded and impoverished to community, which will be enriched by their return.

Throughout Luke's Gospel, Jesus warns against the spiritual and social consequences of building up wealth in this world and ignoring the poor. In the parable of the Rich Man and Lazarus (Luke 16:19-31), the rich man ends up in the hell of alienation from God not because he was wealthy but because he ignored the poor man, Lazarus, at his gate. The landowner who enjoys a bumper harvest (forgetting that the fruits of the earth are a gift from God) and decides to accumulate wealth by building bigger barns, denying the surrounding community access to the harvest, is described by God in unusually strong terms as a "fool!" (Luke 12:20). Jesus the master teacher sums it up in a way his hearers never forgot: "You cannot serve God and wealth" (Luke 16:13). Throughout Luke's Gospel, the accumulation of wealth is condemned as an unjust distribution of resources, which sustains injustice and causes spiritual atrophy in the person who is devoted to wealth.

I don't think we should read the teaching of Jesus in Luke's Gospel as an invitation to be poor (although poverty of spirit, a childlike simplicity of faith before God, is to be striven for). The material poverty and exclusion that kill and demean are not part of God's plan for human flourishing. The main thrust of the teaching is not to get attached to wealth but to share it, so that everyone might have enough, because "where your treasure is, there your heart will be also" (Luke 12:34). The heart that is attached to wealth will harden. The point of selling your possessions and giving alms (Luke 12:33) is not to become poor but to become fully human, to find yourself, by ensuring that everyone has enough to live in dignity. Attachment to wealth is a kind of idolatry and leads to what Pope Francis calls indifference to the poor:

> The great danger in today's world, pervaded as it is by consumerism, is the desolation and anguish born of a complacent yet covetous heart, the feverish pursuit of frivolous pleasures, and a blunted conscience. Whenever our interior life becomes caught up in its own interests and concerns, there is no longer room for others, no place for the poor.[2]

We are called to a new way of life in which we are liberated from the sin of the world, the sin of selfish grasping and possessiveness. We are called into renewed relationship with God (*prayer*), neighbour (*almsgiving*) and creation (*fasting*, consuming no more than we need). In the parable of the Good Samaritan, we are called to an expanded definition of neighbour. In fact, we are called to an expanded definition of ourselves. Who is my neighbour is not the point. The focus is turned back on us: it's about *being a neighbour*, to everybody. We are called to a universal love, not just to love those near and dear to us, but to love our enemies, "expecting nothing in return" (Luke 6:35). In other words, love everybody. This is only possible by the grace of God. This is more than a feeling; it is, as we've said before, a virtue, something you habitually do for the good of the other. Love is a problem for those in power who are motivated by rivalry and vengeance, lording it over others, excluding and exploiting. Love is a threat to power, since it is fundamentally about equality; it seeks to restore everyone to dignity and belonging, to end demeaning poverty and injustice.

For more than half of Luke's Gospel, Jesus is heading to Jerusalem, the religious and political centre, with courageous determination. When he arrives, he is welcomed by enthusiastic crowds. The following day (after a curious incident that we'll look at in Chapter Ten), he heads for the Temple and drives out those who are "selling things" (Luke 19:45). He wants the Temple to be a house of prayer. The religious authorities, threatened by God's prophet, "kept looking for a way to kill him" (19:47). They find a way, of course, in collusion with the Roman authorities, and Jesus is crucified, a violent and degrading form of public execution reserved for slaves and rebels. Jesus, the Word of God, is killed by the powers of the world. He absorbs the violence of the world, the sin of the world, without resistance (1 Peter 2:20-25). As he is dying on the cross, in a moment of extraordinary power, Jesus prays for his executioners, for all the children of Adam and Eve: "Father, forgive them; for they do not know what they are doing" (Luke 23:34).

We are reconciled to God, set free from sin and its consequences, by the death and resurrection of Jesus. The risen Jesus commissions his disciples to go out and preach "repentance and the forgiveness of sins" (24:47), to baptise people into a new life, a new creation. We're called to change our minds and hearts, to build up a different kind of kingdom: a kingdom of peace, love and justice.

Our salvation is not just a private matter. The *Compendium* tells us that "God in Christ redeems not only the individual person but also the social relations existing between men [and women]".[3] The communities of the Church that gather together in the Holy Spirit around the Risen Lord are "catalysts for the redemption and transformation of social relationships".[4] The focus is on the restoration of just and loving relationships, where no one wants for anything.

We get a glimpse of this in St Luke's account of the early Church, where "all who believed were together and had all things in common; they would sell their possessions and goods and distribute the proceeds to all, as any had need" (Acts 2:44-45). According to the principle of the universal destination of goods, "what is already due in justice is not to be offered as a gift of charity".[5] Those who are in need are only receiving what is due to them. This is not simply a dour exercise in social justice. Luke emphasises the joy of the community. It is a place of learning, encounter, fellowship, solidarity, prayer and the breaking of bread (Acts 2:42). A place where dignity, the image of God, is restored in people. It is a vision that quickly fades as the Church expands, but it's a reminder of what the beginning of the kingdom of God on earth might look like: a redistribution of resources so that no one is in need and no one builds up excessive personal wealth; no one is exploited, no one is stigmatised or excluded.

Questions for individual reflection or group discussion:

How do you react to this vision of a Christian lifestyle and the teaching of Jesus on wealth and possessions? How does this compare with your own experience of the Church? What might this vision look like if it began to take place in your community? Where do you see the need for liberation?

Quotations from sacred scripture and the teaching of the Church:

> "Is not this the fast that I choose:
> to loose the bonds of injustice,
> to undo the thongs of the yoke,
> to let the oppressed go free,
> and to break every yoke?
> Is it not to share your bread with the hungry,
> and bring the homeless poor into your house;
> when you see the naked, to cover them,
> and not to hide yourself from your own kin?"
>
> Isaiah 58:6-7

When he came to Nazareth, where he had been brought up, he went to the synagogue on the sabbath day, as was his custom. He stood up to read, and the scroll of the prophet Isaiah was given to him. He unrolled the scroll and found the place where it was written:

> "The Spirit of the Lord is upon me,
> because he has anointed me to bring good news to the poor.
> He has sent me to proclaim release to the captives
> and recovery of sight to the blind,
> to let the oppressed go free,
> to proclaim the year of the Lord's favour."
>
> Luke 4:16-19

> "Sell your possessions, and give alms. Make purses for yourselves that do not wear out, an unfailing treasure in heaven, where no thief comes near and no moth destroys. For where your treasure is, there your heart will be also."
>
> Luke 12:32-34

"The Church aims at a 'complete form of humanism', that is to say, at the 'liberation from everything that oppresses man' and 'the development of the whole man and of all men'. The Church's social doctrine indicates the path to follow for a society reconciled and in harmony through justice and love, a society that anticipates in history, in a preparatory and prefigurative manner, the 'new heavens and a new earth, where righteousness dwells' (2 Peter 3:13)."

Compendium[6]

"The principle of the universal destination of goods is an invitation to develop an economic vision inspired by moral values that permit people not to lose sight of the origin or purpose of these goods, so as to bring about a world of fairness and solidarity."

Compendium[7]

"Justice is particularly important in the present-day context, where the individual value of the person, his dignity and his rights — despite proclaimed intentions — are seriously threatened by the widespread tendency to make exclusive use of criteria of utility and ownership."

Compendium[8]

References

1. *Compendium of the Social Doctrine of the Church* (London: Bloomsbury, 2004), 24.
2. Pope Francis, *Evangelii Gaudium* ("The Joy of the Gospel"), 2.
3. *Compendium*, 52.
4. *Compendium*, 52.
5. *Compendium*, 184.
6. *Compendium*, 82.
7. *Compendium*, 174.
8. *Compendium*, 202.

CATHOLIC SOCIAL TEACHING: AN OVERVIEW

> ***Topics covered:*** *some of the major themes in the social encyclicals since 1891 – the core principles of Catholic Social Teaching – fundamental Gospel values as reference points – CST as the path to follow for a society reconciled and in harmony through justice and love.*

Catholic Social Teaching is a house built on the foundations of sacred scripture, with the book of Genesis as the bedrock: God made the world and human beings out of love, with the intention that they should live in communion with him, each other and creation. The selfishness of human beings, the desire to grasp and possess that which we do not value as gift (original sin, which leads to personal and social sin), is a breach in the friendship that God offers, a turning away into futility and destruction, a distortion of all our relationships. The CST house, our hope of a better way to live, is furnished by the teaching of the Church and our own experience, or engagement in social analysis and action.

The Church has always been attentive to the social question – the relations between people in society – going back to scripture, the law and prophets of the Old Testament, the Gospels and the good news of Jesus to the poor. The teachings of the Fathers of the Church (influential theologians, bishops and scholars in the early centuries of Christianity) and the Doctors of the Church (also theologians, around the time of the Middle Ages, most famously St Thomas Aquinas) also regarded social questions as important to any expression of Christianity. However, a new path in this tradition opened up with the publication, in 1891, of the social encyclical ***Rerum Novarum*** ("On the Condition of Labour") by Pope Leo XIII. The subsequent social encyclicals from the popes are what is known as Catholic Social Teaching. A brief survey of some of the main encyclicals and themes will hopefully open the door into this rich teaching and encourage you to walk in and have a look around.

In 1891, the chief concern of Pope Leo XIII was the terrible impact of the Industrial Revolution on workers and their families, who often worked and lived in degrading conditions with low pay. The key question of the encyclical is often described as the *labour question* – the relationship between labour and capital. At the end of the nineteenth century, the Church in Europe, or at least the institutional or official Church, was more likely to be seen as a conservative force, on the side of the employers and owners rather than of the workers, and certainly not on the side of the social revolutionaries. In that context, *Rerum Novarum* was something of a breakthrough. The central theme is the just ordering of society. It did not take sides with liberal capitalism or socialism, being critical of the way both could undermine the dignity of the person. It advocated a just wage, the principle of collaboration as opposed to conflict and class struggle as the fundamental means of social change, and the right to join professional associations.

On the fortieth anniversary of *Rerum Novarum*, in 1931, Pope Pius XI published ***Quadragesimo Anno*** ("On the Reconstruction of the Social Order"). The context for this encyclical was the Great Depression, which caused a major loss of confidence in the belief that the market could regulate itself. Pius XI comes out strongly against the free market being left to its own devices: "the right ordering of economic life cannot be left to a free competition of forces".[1] He likened this kind of economic thinking to a poisoned spring from which flows social injustice. This encyclical also introduced the concept of **subsidiarity**, the most just level at which decisions should be made, one of the permanent principles of Catholic Social Teaching, which we will look at more closely in Chapter Seven.

Pope Pius XII did not issue any social encyclicals in his long reign (1939–1958), but his **Christmas Messages** during the Second World War deal with many of the key themes of CST and look ahead to the post-war focus on democracy and human rights rooted in dignity. The United Nations' Universal Declaration of Human Rights, adopted on 10 December 1948, was shaped to a large extent by Catholic intellectuals inspired by the Church's social teaching. The famous Article 1 has clear echoes of this teaching:

> All human beings are born free and equal in dignity and rights. They are endowed with reason and conscience and should act towards one another in a spirit of brotherhood.[2]

The first social encyclical after the war, issued in 1961, was Pope John XXIII's ***Mater et Magistra*** ("Christianity and Social Progress"), on the seventieth anniversary of *Rerum Novarum*. This encyclical reflects a new global awareness in the Church, keen to ensure that the fruits of economic progress are shared in as equal a way as possible among all nations. John XXIII, echoing Pius XI, supports the concept of government intervention for the sake of the common good. The approach of this encyclical is very much an opening up to the world, an invitation to the Church to enter into dialogue with the wider society. In this encyclical we find the introduction of the key method to be used in the application of social teaching to concrete situations: **See-Judge-Act**. We'll look at this more closely in Chapter Ten. John XXIII published one more encyclical, ***Pacem in Terris*** ("Peace on Earth"), in 1963, against the backdrop of the Cold War and the Cuban Missile Crisis. The emphasis here is that justice is the true basis of peace. It is also the first major statement of a human rights position grounded in the dignity of the person. It outlines some of the basic requirements for a fully human life.

The Second Vatican Council, the gathering of all the world's bishops with the pope, met in four sessions from 1962 to 1965. One of the sixteen documents to come out of the Council, ***Gaudium et Spes*** (The Pastoral Constitution on the Church in the Modern World), is considered by many to be the most important document on Catholic Social Teaching in the twentieth century. It is certainly the highest level of the Magisterium, or teaching authority of the Church, since it is the work of all the bishops of the Church in communion with the pope. The focus of this document is the progress of the human person and their flourishing in society, where the relational identity of the person can be fulfilled. It gives us the classic definition of the common good as "the sum of those conditions of social life which allow social groups and their individual members relatively thorough and ready access to their own fulfilment".[3] The document makes it clear that part of the vocation of the Christian is the pursuit of justice in the world by seeking more humane and just conditions of life, promoting human rights, defending dignity and building up the human family.

The next major social encyclical is from Pope Paul VI, who in 1967 issued ***Populorum Progressio*** ("On the Development of Peoples"). In this encyclical, the social question is placed in a global context. One of the main arguments is that economic justice is the road to peace. The pope rejects many of the basic precepts of capitalism, such as unrestricted private property, profit before people, and reliance on free trade in the world's economy. A keynote of this document is development, first of all the development of the person, that is an authentic development which includes the development of the whole person and all people. This is what is known in CST as **integral human development**. What guarantees this authentic development is the "transition from less than human conditions to truly human ones".[4] The transition from material poverty, abuse and exploitation, to access to the necessities of life, then education, culture, commitment to the common good and, our highest vocation, communion with God. It is a liberation from everything that oppresses human beings and prevents flourishing.

Referring back to the book of Genesis, the pope states that "if the earth truly was created to provide man with the necessities of life and the tools for his own progress, it follows that every man has the right to glean what he needs from the earth".[5] With a radical edge that we have not always kept in focus, the pope goes on to state that created goods should flow freely to all and that all other principles – including private property and free trade – are subordinated to this principle, which as we've noted already is the universal destination of goods. On a global scale, richer nations have responsibilities to poorer nations. Paul VI names three major duties:

1. **Mutual solidarity:** the aid that richer nations must give to poorer nations
2. **Social justice:** the rectification of trade relations between strong and weak nations
3. **Universal charity:** the effort to build a more humane world community, where all can give and receive, and where the progress of some is not bought at the expense of others.[6]

The pope stresses that this relationship between rich and poor nations should not be paternalistic, or based on force, as in the past. The goal of the world solidarity he envisages is that all people become "artisans of their destiny"[7] and play an equal and dignified part in constructing a better world.

Pope John Paul II, in his long reign (1978–2005), produced at least three major social encyclicals. In the first, ***Laborem Exercens*** ("On Human Work"), the keynote is the priority of labour over capital and, again with a radical vision that we have allowed to blur out of focus, the right of workers to co-ownership: "On the basis of his work each person is fully entitled to consider himself a part-owner of the great workbench where he is working with everyone else.

A way towards that goal could be found by associating labour with the ownership of capital, as far as possible, and by producing a wide range of intermediate bodies with economic, social and cultural purposes."[8]

John Paul II's second encyclical, ***Sollicitudo Rei Socialis*** ("On Social Concern"), issued in 1987, gave us some of the principles that we regard as central to Catholic Social Teaching. Against a backdrop of the rise of neoliberal economics, which favoured unregulated market activity (not supported in CST), the pope shows concern for the increasing gap between rich and poor and insists that the person should be at the centre of our consideration. He emphasises **solidarity**, more than any other pope, perhaps not surprisingly given the prominence of the workers' Solidarity movement in his native Poland. For John Paul II, solidarity is a virtue, something you repeatedly do, not a vague feeling of compassion, but a determination to commit ourselves to the common good, which is the good of all and each individual because "we are all really responsible for all".[9] The "other" is not to be regarded as an instrument to be exploited, but a neighbour with whom we share in the goods of the earth. The pope develops the concept of structures of sin from liberation theology in South America, the systemic and institutional barriers to social justice. For John Paul II these are rooted in the "all-consuming desire for profit"[10] and "the thirst for power, with the intention of imposing one's will upon others".[11] This thirst for power can be traced back to original sin and that distortion of right relations, which we talked about in Chapter Three.

In his third major social encyclical, ***Centesimus Annus*** ("On the Hundredth Anniversary of *Rerum Novarum*"), issued in 1991, John Paul II is writing in the context of the fall of the Berlin Wall and the defeat of communism. This encyclical is taken by some as an endorsement of free market capitalism, but that reading is not supported by the text. There is a qualified endorsement of capitalism but the same insistence as his predecessors on the need to restrain markets and a strong emphasis on the corrupting influence of consumerism and materialism. The pope insists that "the market be appropriately controlled by the forces of society and the state, so as to guarantee that the basic needs of the whole of society are satisfied".[12] John Paul II also introduces a theme that Pope Francis was to make a key theme of his papacy, namely the climate crisis and the degradation of the earth, our common home. Like Francis, John Paul II links the destruction of the planet with our greed and selfishness: "In his desire to have and to enjoy rather than to be and to grow, man consumes the resources of the earth and his own life in an excessive and disordered way."[13]

Just as *Quadragesimo Anno* was a response to the Great Depression, so ***Caritas in Veritate*** ("On Integral Human Development in Charity and Truth") by Pope Benedict XVI, issued in 2009, was a response to the financial crash of the previous year. One of the key points of this encyclical is that the financial crash was a crisis of ethics, driven by immoral and greedy behaviour. Like his predecessor, Benedict stresses that market regulation is required to protect the marginalised. In connection with this, he also underlines the importance of labour unions to defend the rights of workers and ensure their well-being. The economy cannot be left to its own devices. Justice must be applied to ensure that the needs, and rights, of people are met. The economy is not a value-free zone, but, rather, "every economic decision has a moral consequence".[14] Pope Benedict also reinforces other key themes of CST, such as creation as gift of a loving and generous God and the centrality of relationality to human identity, since we are made in the image of the Trinity, which is absolute loving relationality. This is the source and inspiration for how we live together. This is why seeking the common good – the good of all and the whole person – "is a requirement of justice and charity".[15]

Pope Francis became pope in March 2013, following the resignation of Pope Benedict XVI. Francis has issued two major social encyclicals, ***Laudato Si'*** ("On Care for Our Common Home") in 2015 and ***Fratelli Tutti*** ("On Fraternity and Social Friendship") in 2020. We will look at these encyclicals in greater detail in later chapters, but for now it is enough to say that *Laudato Si'* was a landmark document, the first time an entire social encyclical was devoted to the ecological crisis. Unlike previous documents, it is addressed not just to people in the Catholic Church but to "every person living on this planet".[16] The impact of the document has been felt far beyond the Church. One of its key concerns is to develop an understanding of integral ecology, the belief that everything is connected. When human beings are living life to the full, they are in right relationship with God, neighbour, especially our neighbour who is in poverty, and creation. The pope calls us to a conversion of heart and lifestyle, an ecological conversion. In *Fratelli Tutti*, Pope Francis takes as his theme fraternity, or social friendship. In an age that has seen the return of populism, nationalism, polarisation, fear and suspicion of the stranger, the pope emphasises the urgent need to build bridges, not walls, to overcome the culture of indifference and individualism with new forms of openness and solidarity, the need to shift the culture from *me* to *we*.

The teaching of the social encyclicals has evolved over time. Each is not simply a repetition of what has gone before, but teaching based on a reading of the signs of the times for that particular age. For example, Paul VI's position on private property was stronger than that of his predecessors. He had travelled the world and seen the vast agricultural estates where the labour of many maintained the few in great wealth. He taught that the right to private property was subordinate to the universal destination of goods, the right of everybody to a share of the earth's goods suitable to sustain a decent life. He went as far as to say, "If certain landed estates impede the general prosperity because they are extensive, unused or poorly used, or because they bring hardship to peoples or are detrimental to the interests of the country, the common good sometimes demands their expropriation."[17]

Another example is the teaching of Pope Francis on the economy. We can see here a clear difference from his predecessors. It is no longer about just "toning down" capitalism, or trying to inject some compassion. Pope Francis has come to the conclusion that it's about "redefining our notion of progress"[18]: totally transforming the economic world order. To avoid "dealing merely with symptoms"[19] it is necessary to rethink the entire economic model from the bottom up. Respect for human rights and human dignity "is the preliminary condition for a country's social and economic development".[20] The economy of mere profit does not have the dignity of every person at its heart and so it leads to inequality and exclusion, undermining the common good. For an example of what a new economics based on dignity and the care of our common home might look like, you might like to visit the website of the Economy of Francesco, inspired by a gathering of young economists and change makers at the invitation of Pope Francis in 2022. The final statement can be found at: https://francescoeconomy.org/final-statement-eof-assisi-2022/.

Even in this brief survey of some of the social encyclicals of Catholic Social Teaching, I hope it's become evident that there are common themes that run through the teaching. There are a number of versions of how many key principles there are in CST. In various places, I've seen seven pillars, eight principles, ten themes. None of these versions are wrong as such, but the *Compendium* identifies **four permanent principles** in Catholic Social Teaching: **the dignity of the human person**, which is the foundation of all the other principles, **solidarity**, **subsidiarity** and **the common good**. These are the main reference points for interpreting and evaluating social realities, for reading the signs of the times. They are rooted in the Gospel mandate to love God and neighbour in justice.

It is worth remembering that the *Compendium* was published in 2004, more than ten years before *Laudato Si'* in 2015. I would suggest that when the *Compendium* is updated there is a very strong case for making **Care of Our Common Home** a fifth permanent principle of Catholic Social Teaching. There are some who would argue that, given the existential threat to life on the planet, this is more than just a theme of CST, but ***the*** point of reference. I will proceed with a thematic approach, which I think is more helpful for those in schools and parishes trying to make Catholic Social Teaching central to the culture. There are many dimensions of the permanent principles, which help to give the fuller picture of the themes of this teaching (see the diagram at the end of this chapter). The permanent principles should always be appreciated in their unity and interconnectedness. A focus on one of the principles in isolation can lead to a distorted view. One group of people, for example, might argue for power and influence in the name of subsidiarity, but this needs to be balanced by the impact on the dignity of the person, the good of all, and the environment.

These principles are inspired by what the *Compendium* calls fundamental values, or "social values".[21] These values are our points of reference for "the proper structuring and ordered leading of life in society",[22] a society more in conformity with God's will for his creation. These values are **truth, freedom, justice and love**. If you look back at Chapter Four and our consideration of the Nazareth Manifesto in Luke's Gospel, you'll see those values indicated by the proclamation of Jesus. Putting these values into practice is the sure way of obtaining our salvation, our destiny as human beings, but also a "more human social existence".[23] To make these values a reality requires the personal exercise of virtue, which we'll look at in Chapter Ten.

Another approach to CST, apart from beginning with a consideration of the permanent principles, is to work through the entire body of social encyclicals. This might be called the scholarly approach, since only scholars are likely to have the time and need to do this. For most people, that would be a daunting task. Another approach might be called the partisan approach, when one has a favourite pope or encyclical and starts from there. For example, as mentioned above, some (wrongly, in my view) believe that Pope John Paul II's *Centesimus Annus* was the Church's endorsement of capitalism and that's their go-to encyclical. Another approach might be called a hermeneutics of the signs of the times; in other words, being attentive to Magisterial teaching beginning with the encyclical that most recently addresses the challenges we are facing at this moment in history. That would mean (at the time of writing) beginning with *Fratelli Tutti* by Pope Francis and viewing the tradition through that lens. I would add to that approach to keep in mind the importance of Vatican II's *Gaudium et Spes*, as the Church's highest teaching authority on social doctrine.

Catholic Social Teaching, as inspired by our divine origin and shared humanity, can be seen as showing the way towards the common good, the flourishing of all. It is important to remember, however, that the common good of society is not an end in itself. This is not just a social or historical project. We have an eternal destiny: God is our ultimate end, our beatitude, our final common good as a human race. "The Church's social doctrine indicates the path to follow for a society reconciled and in harmony through justice and love, a society that anticipates in history, in a preparatory and prefigurative manner, the 'new heavens and a new earth in which righteousness dwells' (2 Peter 3:13)."[24] This path, this collective effort to elevate the human condition, begins and ends in Jesus and has a transcendent goal. In this life, we see its prefigurement. It is a path, you could say, from sin to grace, in other words:

- From **me**... to **we**
- From **them**... to **us**
- From **indifference**... to **solidarity**
- From **isolation**... to **participation**
- From **exploitation**... to **agency**
- From **greed**... to **gift**
- From **extraction**... to **stewardship**
- From **what I want**... to **what God's world needs**
- From **throwaway**... to **cherished**
- From **enmity**... to **reconciliation**
- From **passivity**... to **advocacy**
- From **poverty**... to **dignity**
- From **enclaves**... to **communion**

This path begins in compassion, the heart of the Gospel, but does not end there. It ends with justice and fellowship. Everything on the left is the old world, what St Paul calls the Old Adam: futility, vanity, greed, the lust to dominate. It's going nowhere. It's death. The truth that CST witnesses to is a different story of what it is to be human and to belong in community. On the right is the New Adam, the prefiguring of the reign of God, the new creation. We see this transition all the time in the Gospels, as Jesus leads people from blindness to sight, from exclusion to inclusion, from sin to forgiveness, from sickness to health, from being bound down to being set free, from death to life.

We don't get there by accident. Justice doesn't just fall from the sky. It's an intentional struggle. Nor is this transition or transformation the result of our will, or our efforts. That is known as Pelagianism. This transformation is the result of the grace of God working in us, working in the Church, working in the world. To the extent that we co-operate with grace, which is always seeking our good, we will bring about this transformation. Catholicism is not, as Marx suggested, an opiate to dull us into passivity and acceptance of the status quo, although his insight was not without some foundation in truth at the time. Catholicism, as Vatican II tells us, is a stimulant:

> Therefore, while we are warned that it profits a man nothing if he gain the whole world and lose himself, the expectation of a new earth must not weaken but rather stimulate our concern for cultivating this one. For here grows the body of a new human family, a body which even now is able to give some kind of foreshadowing of the new age.[25]

Questions for individual reflection or group discussion:

Do any themes or ideas from the tradition of Catholic Social Teaching surprise or challenge you? Do you feel you're developing an understanding of the "big picture" of CST, what it's all about? Can you try to express that in a few lines, or share it with the group?

Quotations from sacred scripture and the teaching of the Church:

> "Now there are varieties of gifts, but the same Spirit; and there are varieties of services, but the same Lord; and there are varieties of activities, but it is the same God who activates all of them in everyone. To each is given the manifestation of the Spirit for the common good."
>
> 1 Corinthians 12:4-7

> "The mission of the Catholic Church, under the guidance of the Holy Spirit, is to carry on the work of Jesus, 'who came into the world to give witness to the truth, to save and not to judge, to serve and not to be served'."
>
> *Gaudium et Spes*[26]

"Just as Christ carried out the work of redemption in poverty and persecution, so the Church is called to follow the same route that it might communicate the fruits of salvation to men. Christ Jesus, 'though He was by nature God... emptied Himself, taking the nature of a slave', and 'being rich, became poor'[78] for our sakes. Thus, the Church, although it needs human resources to carry out its mission, is not set up to seek earthly glory, but to proclaim, even by its own example, humility and self-sacrifice. Christ was sent by the Father 'to bring good news to the poor, to heal the contrite of heart',[79] 'to seek and to save what was lost'.[80] Similarly, the Church encompasses with love all who are afflicted with human suffering and in the poor and afflicted sees the image of its poor and suffering Founder. It does all it can to relieve their need and in them it strives to serve Christ."

Lumen Gentium[27]

"By means of her social doctrine, the Church shows her concern for human life in society, aware that the quality of social life – that is, of the relationships of justice and love that form the fabric of society – depends in a decisive manner on the protection and promotion of the human person, for whom every community comes into existence. In fact, at play in society are the dignity and rights of the person, and peace in the relationships between persons and between communities of persons. These are goods that the social community must pursue and guarantee. In this perspective, the Church's social doctrine has the task of *proclamation*, but also of *denunciation*."

Compendium[28]

References

1. Pope Pius XI, *Quadragesimo Anno* ("On the Reconstruction of the Social Order"), 88.
2. Universal Declaration of Human Rights, https://www.un.org/en/about-us/universal-declaration-of-human-rights, accessed 29 April 2023.
3. Second Vatican Council, *Gaudium et Spes* (The Pastoral Constitution on the Church in the Modern World), 26.
4. Pope Paul VI, *Populorum Progressio* ("On the Development of Peoples"), 20.
5. *Populorum Progressio*, 22.
6. *Populorum Progressio*, 44.
7. *Populorum Progressio*, 65.
8. Pope John Paul II, *Laborem Exercens* ("On Human Work"), 14.
9. Pope John Paul II, *Sollicitudo Rei Socialis* ("On Social Concern"), 38.
10. *Sollicitudo Rei Socialis*, 37.
11. *Sollicitudo Rei Socialis*, 37.
12. Pope John Paul II, *Centesimus Annus* ("On the Hundredth Anniversary of *Rerum Novarum*"), 35.
13. *Centesimus Annus*, 37.
14. Pope Benedict XVI, *Caritas in Veritate* ("On Integral Human Development in Charity and Truth"), 37.
15. *Caritas in Veritate*, 7.
16. Pope Francis, *Laudato Si'* ("On Care for Our Common Home"), 3.
17. *Populorum Progressio*, 24.
18. Pope Francis, *Laudato Si'*, 194.
19. *Laudato Si'*, 9.
20. *Fratelli Tutti*, 22.
21. *Compendium of the Social Doctrine of the Church*, (London: Bloomsbury, 2004), 197.
22. *Compendium*, 197.
23. *Compendium*, 197.
24. *Compendium*, 82.
25. *Gaudium et Spes*, 39.
26. *Gaudium et Spes*, 3.
27. Second Vatican Council, *Lumen Gentium* (Dogmatic Constitution on the Church), 8.
28. *Compendium*, 81.

CATHOLIC SOCIAL TEACHING
Permanent Principles

DIVINE ORIGIN

↓

DIGNITY

Everyone is loved and capable of love - right to life - human rights and duties - dignity of workers - right to the goods of the earth

↓

SOLIDARITY

Think of the needs of others - all are responsible for all - one human family - service - work for justice

↓

SUBSIDIARITY

Everyone has a say, especially the marginalised - participation - associations and groups - decisions at lowest level possible, highest level necessary

↓

CARE FOR OUR COMMON HOME

Conversion of the heart - cry of the earth, cry of the poor - integral ecology - live simply - education - stewardship - divestment

↓

COMMON GOOD

Flourishing of all - preferential option for the poor - family - responsibility - community - discernment - social justice - peace - civilisation of love

↓

ETERNAL DESTINY

THE DIGNITY OF THE PERSON: A TRULY HUMAN LIFE

> ***Topics covered:*** *the principle of the dignity of the human person – dignity in the Gospel – the right to life – the concept of freedom – dignity as socially entrusted – challenging where there is not dignity in our society.*

In St John's Gospel, there's a scene of high tension in the grounds of the Temple in Jerusalem. Jesus was sitting before a crowd, the posture of a teacher in the ancient world. We don't know what he was teaching them, since he was interrupted by an indignant group of scribes and Pharisees, the religious elite of the day. They had brought with them a woman, "caught in the very act of committing adultery" (John 8:4). The temperature suddenly rises, the crowd stirs; at the heart of this commotion is a woman who has been forcibly taken by a group of men to face a reckoning. The Jewish Law (Torah) says that such a woman should be stoned to death (Leviticus 20:10). It also says that the man should be put to death, but there's no sign of him. They've singled out the woman who has been *caught-brought-made to stand* in front of them all: the language of coercion and domination.

The woman is held in the stony stare of the religious elite, condemned. They don't see a woman, but a sinner, a category, an object of their power plays. They can't find anything against Jesus to put him in the middle of their self-righteous stare, so they try to trap him in this way, using a frightened, dishevelled woman as their prop. The law says that this woman should be stoned to death, they remind Jesus. What does he say? Jesus takes his time, mysteriously writing on the ground. If he agrees to the stoning, he'll be in trouble with the Romans, who had a fortress overlooking the Temple and always kept a close eye on what was going on. The Romans did not permit execution by stoning for adultery. If he refuses the stoning, it will look as if he disagrees with the law of Moses and he'll be in trouble with the religious authorities.

Jesus has a genius for side-stepping traps like this. Instead of answering their question, he says, "Let anyone among you who is without sin be the first to throw a stone at her" (8:7). He holds a mirror up to them. He breaks their spell of fake goodness. They all know they have sinned, but are not willing to step into the new life Jesus is offering and receive forgiveness, the path to a new way of being human. They prefer to stay in their enclave of superiority and judgement. The stones drop out of their hands; one by one they leave, beginning with the eldest, the one who knows more than anybody his history of sin. They all leave, and Jesus is alone with the woman. He did not come to humiliate people, to stone them, or condemn them. He asks the woman, "Has no one condemned you?" (8:10). "No one," answers the woman. "Neither do I condemn you. Go your way, and from now on do not sin again" (8:11).

Pope Francis, referring to this scene, says that Jesus "anoints her with dignity".[1] That's why people followed Jesus. He gave them dignity. "For Jesus," says the pope, "every person is capable of dignity and has value. Jesus restores the true worth of each person and the people as a whole because He can see with God's eyes: 'God saw that it was good' (Genesis 1:10)."[2] This was not the mindset of the religious elites, who controlled the "goods" of religion and access to God. They judged and exploited the vulnerable, "They devour widows' houses" (Mark 12:40; Luke 20:47), decided who was worthy and who was not. Jesus, on the other hand, walked with the exploited ones, the excluded ones, the ones declared outside the law. He brought God close to the people. He challenged the mindset that builds identity on closed groups, identifying scapegoats to unify around fake goodness, and "builds walls to dominate and exclude".[3] This is the second great foundation of human dignity: not only are we made in God's image, but God became one of us and dignified for ever the human condition. When God became flesh in Jesus, he made it his mission to seek out the lost, the least and the last, to restore dignity to the poor and excluded. More radically still, Jesus challenges us to see his presence in the most vulnerable and marginalised – the hungry, the sick, the prisoner, the stranger – when he says that whatever we did to them, "you did it to me" (Matthew 25:40).

In the ancient Roman world, dignity, or *dignitas*, was a quality attributed only to men and related to their reputation, achievements and honour. It was not something you were born with, although being born into an aristocratic family was a good start. It was conferred, gained and upheld by society. It could also be lost, which was why it was zealously protected. We have traces of this approach today when we talk about dignitaries, or VIPs, by implication people with more worth (L. *dignus*) than other people: the people we roll out the red carpet for, reserve the best seats for, the ones who don't have to queue like the rest of us. At the heart of the Judeo-Christian tradition is an idea that changed the world: every human being has an inherent dignity because they are made in the image and likeness of God (Genesis 1:27). This dignity is the source of their rights as well as their duties. This dignity is something that cannot be lost, although it can be debased, so we all have a role in its protection and promotion. This is the foundational concept of Catholic Social Teaching.

Cardinal Basil Hume, writing in the Preface to the 1996 document *The Common Good* from the Catholic Bishops' Conference of England and Wales, states that "in virtue simply of our shared humanity, we must surely respect and honour one another. Each individual has a value that can never be lost and must never be ignored. Moreover, each of us is made in the image and likeness of God. Society must therefore first of all respect and protect human life itself – at all stages from conception to its natural end."[4] The Church has consistently witnessed to the dignity of the human person throughout the life course. In some accounts of CST, the protection of the dignity of the unborn is muted, but this is not true to our tradition. As Pope Francis says, "we find it difficult to make people see that when we raise other questions less palatable to public opinion, we are doing so out of fidelity to precisely the same convictions about human dignity and the common good".[5] Nor is it true to the Catholic tradition if protection of the unborn is the *only* issue that is promoted in defence of human dignity.

The late Cardinal Joseph Bernadin of Chicago was well known for advancing the concept of a *consistent life ethic*, in other words an attitude of profound respect for and defence of the sanctity of human life at every moment of its duration. Cardinal Bernadin often used the biblical metaphor of the seamless garment. Pope Francis takes up the same theme when he states that the Church's defence of the innocent unborn is clear and firm, "for at stake is the dignity of a human life".[6] He goes on to say that "equally sacred, however, are the lives of the poor, those already born, the destitute, the abandoned and the underprivileged, the vulnerable infirm and elderly exposed to covert euthanasia, the victims of trafficking, new forms of slavery, and every form of rejection".[7]

When we talk about being made in the image of God, it is important to remember that we are talking about being made in the image of the Trinity, in other words a relational and loving God of three equal persons: the Father, Son and Holy Spirit. Our dignity, our fullness as human beings, is in being relational: with God, our neighbour, and creation. We have the self-knowledge and the freedom to mature in these relationships, or to turn away from them, but we will always be aware somewhere in our hearts that there is something beyond us, bigger than us. As it says in *Gaudium et Spes*, we bear within us the "seed of eternity".[8] Our dignity is served by being able to live a fully human life in society, without the fear of oppression or exploitation, but it is most fully realised in our relationship with the transcendent Creator.

When we say that part of our dignity is our freedom, there is a divergence between what the Church says about freedom and what secular society says. In a secular discourse, freedom is freedom from any form of indoctrination or oppression, often associated in the past with the Church and hierarchical authority. It is freedom to choose, to be "myself", including choices over one's identity and body. It is the freedom of the consumer, a freedom which can only be realised, of course, if you have the means. Hence, many people are left in a state of unfulfilled desire, envy and anxiety. In these terms, dignity is about self-reliance, self-determination, responsibility for forging my own path. In the tradition of CST, freedom is certainly freedom from the oppression of various types of poverty, since poverty undermines dignity. It's also freedom from selfishness, or in more traditional language, freedom from slavery to sin, from following my own impulses and external pressures. Our freedom to turn to God, to respond in love with the help of God's grace, is our greatest dignity, because it is our deepest identity. We attain the fullest sense of who we are in being loving, "in sincere self-giving".[9]

Catholic Social Teaching also insists that social conditions are part of our dignity. Anna Rowlands, in her reflections on this theme,[10] makes the connection between dignity and the universal destination of goods. *Gaudium et Spes* states that "God has destined the earth and all it contains for the use of everyone and of all peoples, so that the good things of creation should be available equally to all, with justice as guide and charity in attendance".[11] If Catholic Social Teaching is the Church's best-kept secret, then this is the best-kept secret in CST. No wonder, as it is so radical. *Gaudium et Spes* – the highest teaching authority of the Church, remember – goes on to say that "a person who is living in extreme need has the right to procure from the riches of others what is necessary for personal sustenance".[12] All other rights are secondary to this, including the right to private property. We do not have an absolute right to possessions if others are in want. As Rowlands says, we are called to steward the goods of the earth well, so that the needs of all are met. Simple, radical, difficult.

Another facet of dignity that Rowlands brings out in the film clip is that dignity is socially entrusted. In other words, I entrust my dignity to you and you entrust it to me. For those who are not able to realise their dignity for themselves, such as the young, the sick, the very old, we have a role in helping to realise their dignity. We are shocked and repulsed when we hear of the mistreatment of the young, the sick, the very old. Their dignity is in our hands and when we fail them, we know it is not right. This is the result of our conscience, the place where God speaks to us about what is right and wrong. *Gaudium et Spes* also uses the metaphor of leaven, the catalysing agent that causes bread to rise: "The leaven of the gospel has stimulated and stimulates in the human heart the irresistible demands of dignity."[13] Christian realism also reminds us that this is not the case all the time in everyone. Consciences can be blunted; the inner voice of God can be ignored, until over time it ceases to be heard.

The final facet of dignity highlighted by Rowlands is that it requires action. It is more than just a quality we possess and admire. It is an attribute that can be degraded by other people and by institutional structures. Our commitment to dignity is personal and structural; in other words, it is compassion *and* justice, as we said in Chapter One. We can help with our time and talent in our own community, in our family, in all our encounters, but there is a bigger picture to attend to. Pope Francis teaches in *Fratelli Tutti* that "it is an act of charity to assist someone suffering, but it is also an act of charity, even if we do not know that person, to work to change the social conditions that caused his or her suffering".[14] On a structural level, we can name the threats to dignity: in the benefits system, the immigration system, the prison system, the terms and conditions of workers. We can organise to apply pressure for change. More locally, in a school or a parish, we can ask the same questions: where is there not dignity? In what places, on what occasions, is dignity threatened? In the lunch queue, the changing rooms, on the journey home?

What external pressures are at work in society to undermine and insult human dignity? In a school setting, teachers are well aware of the huge pressure from social media on young people to conform to a particular version of beauty or sexual attractiveness. In the 2022 report from The Children's Society, *The Good Childhood Report*,[15] the findings showed that what young people were most unhappy about was their appearance. The relentless narrative of social media is telling them *you're not good enough*. This is not just the vicious opinion of a few individuals. Behind this message there are huge commercial interests preying on the low self-esteem they have manufactured, offering solutions like physical interventions, chemical fixes, supplements, self-help and fitness programmes to help the young person conform to the image of perfection they have promoted. Social media influencers fund their wealth by advertising various products. The global plastic surgery and procedures market is a multi-billion-dollar industry, projected to grow exponentially in the coming years. There is a malign undercurrent to all this in the form of misogyny, which, in the terms used by Pope Francis, seeks "to possess and exploit that which we do not value as gift".[16] It is another form of extracting value from where it should not be taken, in this case from our young people.

When the threats we face are viewed through the lens of Catholic Social Teaching, we can begin to discern a Gospel-inspired call to action. The indignity of poverty is a failure to structure society so as to share the goods of creation to which all are entitled in an equitable way; the ecological crisis likewise is a failure to live simply with what we need for a decent life: it is the greed of wanting to consume in a way that cannot be universalised; the dramatic increase in domestic abuse and misogynistic behaviour is a failure to honour the equal dignity of men and women in relationship; the rapid spread of the zero-hours-contract culture and subsequent in-work poverty is a failure to protect the dignity of workers, with the value generated by labour flowing mostly to the owners. The priority of labour over capital, or people before profits, has been a key theme of CST from the beginning.

The foundational principle of CST is also a call to action in defence of the dignity of the human person wherever their dignity is under threat and, moreover, a call to work to change the conditions that make such indignity possible. As we continue on our path towards a society reconciled in harmony and justice, we will consider the role played by our next two permanent principles: solidarity and subsidiarity.

Questions for individual reflection or group discussion:

Do you believe that we uphold the dignity of some in our society more than others? In your own experience, or setting, can you identify occasions or places where the dignity of some is not upheld? If we are committed to a preferential option for the poor, are we prepared to invite those who are most disadvantaged in our setting to a conversation about perceptions of dignity? What else can we do to promote and protect dignity?

Quotations from sacred scripture and the teaching of the Church:

> "For it was you who formed my inward parts;
> you knit me together in my mother's womb.
> I praise you, for I am fearfully and wonderfully made."
>
> Psalm 139:13-14

> "Do you not know that you are God's temple and that God's Spirit dwells in you?"
>
> 1 Corinthians 3:16

"Rejoice with those who rejoice, weep with those who weep. Live in harmony with one another; do not be haughty, but associate with the lowly; do not claim to be wiser than you are. Do not repay anyone evil for evil, but take thought for what is noble in the sight of all."

Romans 12:15-17

"Wealthy owners and all masters of labour should be mindful of this: that to exercise pressure upon the indigent and the destitute for the sake of gain, and to gather one's profit out of the need of another, is condemned by all laws, human and divine."

Rerum Novarum[17]

"There is a growing awareness of the exalted dignity proper to the human person, since he stands above all things, and his rights and duties are universal and inviolable. Therefore, there must be made available to all men everything necessary for leading a life truly human, such as food, clothing, and shelter; the right to choose a state of life freely and to found a family, the right to education, to employment, to a good reputation, to respect, to appropriate information, to activity in accord with the upright norm of one's own conscience, to protection of privacy and rightful freedom even in matters religious."

Gaudium et Spes[18]

"What is meant by the word 'decent' in regard to work? It means work that expresses the essential dignity of every man and woman in the context of their particular society: work that is freely chosen, effectively associating workers, both men and women, with the development of their community;

work that enables the worker to be respected and free from any form of discrimination; work that makes it possible for families to meet their needs and provide schooling for their children, without the children themselves being forced into labour; work that permits the workers to organize themselves freely, and to make their voices heard; work that leaves enough room for rediscovering one's roots at a personal, familial and spiritual level; work that guarantees those who have retired a decent standard of living."

Caritas in Veritate[19]

"The world exists for everyone, because all of us were born with the same dignity. Differences of colour, religion, talent, place of birth or residence, and so many others, cannot be used to justify the privileges of some over the rights of all. As a community, we have an obligation to ensure that every person lives with dignity and has sufficient opportunities for his or her integral development."

Pope Francis[20]

"Every human being has the right to live with dignity and to develop integrally; this fundamental right cannot be denied by any country. People have this right even if they are unproductive, or were born with or developed limitations. This does not detract from their great dignity as human persons, a dignity based not on circumstances but on the intrinsic worth of their being. Unless this basic principle is upheld, there will be no future either for fraternity or for the survival of humanity."

Pope Francis[21]

> "The Catholic school loses its purpose without constant reference to the Gospel and a frequent encounter with Christ. It derives all the energy necessary for its educational work from Him and thus 'creates in the school community an atmosphere permeated with the Gospel spirit of freedom and love'. In this setting the pupil experiences his or her dignity as a person before he or she knows its definition."
>
> Congregation for Catholic Education[22]

The voice of the lived experience of poverty

Martin Green is a lone parent who lives in Halifax. Unable to work, he has found again and again that the benefits system – which should act as an anchor for people like Martin and his children – has instead swept them further into poverty:

> The amount paid in benefits means you're facing impossible situations. In a good month I can get stuff for food but never anything extra. If I need a new pair of shoes, for example, I need to take money off what I have for food…
>
> I just snack; I don't eat proper meals. The children have always come first and I just eat small bits here and there. I sometimes go all day without eating. If my lad is out with his mates, I will sometimes not eat… If I'm in the house on my own all day I'll tend not to eat until 6 or 7 o'clock, if at all, and I know that if I can keep that food in the cupboard a bit longer, that's another day of survival.
>
> Because I am in the church circle, I have a lot of charitable friends who are helping me. I'm okay for being fed but I have no money to do anything with my sons, like go out to the cinema or football. That's what's the hardest thing for me.[23]

References

1. Pope Francis, *Let Us Dream* (London: Simon & Schuster, 2020), 123.
2. *Let Us Dream*, 124.
3. *Let Us Dream*, 124.
4. Catholic Bishops' Conference of England and Wales, *The Common Good*, 1.
5. Pope Francis, *Evangelii Gaudium* ("The Joy of the Gospel"), 65.
6. Pope Francis, *Gaudete et Exsultate* ("On the Call to Holiness in Today's World"), 101.
7. *Gaudete et Exsultate*, 101.
8. Second Vatican Council, *Gaudium et Spes* (Pastoral Constitution on the Church in the Modern World), 18.
9. *Gaudium et Spes*, 24.
10. Anna Rowlands on Catholic Social Teaching and Dignity, https://www.youtube.com/watch?v=HS7Y2ErFRJU, accessed 30 April 2023.
11. *Gaudium et Spes*, 69.
12. *Gaudium et Spes*, 69.
13. *Gaudium et Spes*, 26.
14. Pope Francis, *Fratelli Tutti* ("On Fraternity and Social Friendship"), 186.
15. The Children's Society, *The Good Childhood Report 2022*, https://www.childrenssociety.org.uk/information/professionals/resources/good-childhood-report-2022, accessed 30 April 2023.
16. *Let Us Dream*, 34.
17. *Rerum Novarum*, 20.
18. *Gaudium et Spes*, 26.
19. Pope Benedict XVI, *Caritas in Veritate*, 63.
20. Pope Francis, *Fratelli Tutti*, 118.
21. *Fratelli Tutti*, 107.
22. Congregation for Catholic Education, *The Catholic School*, 55.
23. Church Action on Poverty, https://www.church-poverty.org.uk/stories/speaking-truth-to-power/, accessed 4 June 2023.

SOLIDARITY AND SUBSIDIARITY: PATHWAYS TO THE COMMON GOOD

> ***Topics covered:*** *the Good Samaritan – solidarity as being a neighbour – solidarity as a moral virtue opposed to structures of sin – solidarity as service and working to change the structural causes of poverty – subsidiarity as decision making at the most appropriate level – subsidiarity as a voice for those who are most disadvantaged.*

"And who is my neighbour?" (Luke 10:29). Another tricky question for Jesus, this time from a lawyer. The stakes are not as high as in the encounter between Jesus and the scribes and Pharisees in the Temple, with an edgy Roman army looking on, but how he chooses to answer is still significant. If Jesus defines who is included in the concept of neighbour, then he's also defining who is *not* included. Every time you make a group you make a small "us", which is defined in opposition to who is not in the group, usually a larger "them". A lot of energy can then go into protecting and promoting the boundary markers of the group and keeping the rest outside. Jesus avoids this trap, as he avoids most traps. This time, his response is to tell a story, a parable.

It's the one about the man who was going down the steep road from Jerusalem to Jericho, a dangerous, dusty road, with twists and turns and rocky places for robbers to lie in wait. He is set upon by a gang, beaten, stripped, robbed and left for dead. There he lies in the heat and silence, devoid of all identity markers: his clothes, his accent, his goods. He is, if you like, a symbol of the fallen human being, utterly vulnerable, with no hope of recovery on his own. He will die soon, alone. But now, "by chance" (10:31), somebody is coming. It is often by chance that we encounter people in need, or come upon a situation where we could make a difference. The priest who comes along sees the man, but passes by on the other side, with a "nervous indifference".[1] There's too much at stake here; he's more concerned about himself than about the fallen one. Same goes for the Levite, another religious official, who comes along next and also passes by.

Then along comes the Samaritan. At that point in the story, there may well have been groans from the crowd, boos from the back, maybe even a contemptuous spit. The Jews regarded Samaritans as unclean, bad neighbours, people who were beyond their care. Jesus has a habit of turning things upside down. He makes the Samaritan the hero of his story. He is the one who "came near" (10:33) the victim and when he saw him "he was moved with pity" (10:33). The Greek word for pity is *esplanchnisthé*. It means to be moved in your inmost parts, a deep reaction of compassion in your emotional centre. It's the same word used to describe the reaction of Jesus to the Widow of Nain as she buries her only son (Luke 7:13), or the reaction of Jesus to the lost and bedraggled crowd, like sheep without a shepherd (Mark 6:34). It is the response of God to human suffering and precarity. The compassion of God runs through the insides of the Good Samaritan like an express train. He drew near to the wounded man "and bandaged his wounds" (10:34). The Gospel begins with compassion, which prompts action.

Pope Francis devotes an entire chapter of his social encyclical, *Fratelli Tutti*, to the story of the Good Samaritan. For the pope, this story gives us a ray of light in dark times, a horizon of hope in a world that is closed in on itself and tends to cross to the other side to avoid human weakness and suffering. In what Pope Francis calls a "culture of walls",[2] there's an increasing tendency to look after myself and my group and not risk any encounter with those outside that group. This is the opposite of solidarity: this is polarisation, division, indifference. **Solidarity** is founded on the principle that "as a human family we have our common origin in God; we live in a common home, the garden-planet, the earth where God placed us; and we have a common destination in Christ".[3] For the Samaritan, there was no calculation of who was worthy of his care or not, just a recognition that a fellow human being needed help. Solidarity is stepping out of our safe space to help another in need, because their need is our need.

Solidarity is a moral virtue, something you do, not just a principle you admire. John Paul II, in his social encyclical, *Sollicitudo Rei Socialis*, says that solidarity is not just a feeling of vague compassion, but rather "a firm and persevering determination to commit oneself to the common good; that is to say the good of all and of each individual, because we are all really responsible for all".[4] The barriers to solidarity and the common good, according to John Paul II, are what he calls the desire for profit and thirst for power. These result in "structures of sin"[5]: embedded practices in institutions and systems, which undermine the dignity of the person, discriminate against certain groups and advance the power and benefits of the few.

These structures of sin and their baleful effects are only conquered by their opposite, structures of solidarity, the commitment to the good of one's neighbour and a readiness, with the help of God's grace, "to lose oneself for the sake of the other instead of exploiting him, and to 'serve him' instead of oppressing him for one's own advantage".[6] Solidarity helps us to see the other not as a threat, or a problem, but as my sister or brother. John Paul II places the preferential option for the poor at the heart of our commitment to solidarity. The Church is called "to take her stand beside the poor, to discern the justice of their requests and to satisfy them".[7] We can see how the principles of CST interweave. Solidarity is based on the foundational principle of the dignity of the person, especially the most vulnerable, and our fulfilment as relational loving beings in community, building the common good. Nobody is beyond our care; no one should be excluded or cast aside.

Pope Francis tells us that the parable of the Good Samaritan calls us to decision. There is nowhere to hide. In the face of so much suffering and division, we either imitate the Good Samaritan or we are one of the robbers, or one of the ones who walked by. Indifference is the ally of injustice, especially structures of sin, which will never reform themselves. The parable shows us an alternative to disengagement, how community can be rebuilt by men and women who identify with the vulnerability of others, "who reject the creation of a society of exclusion, and act instead as neighbours, lifting up and rehabilitating the fallen for the sake of the common good".[8] We are called to build a culture of encounter instead of a culture of walls, a culture of closeness and care instead of a culture of violence, coldness and cynicism: "Isolation, no; closeness, yes; Culture wars, no; culture of encounter, yes".[9]

The Good Samaritan gave the wounded man his time. He allowed himself to be interrupted and, at some risk to himself (were the robbers still nearby?), treated the man with skill and attention, using his own resources, pouring oil and wine (the disinfectants of the ancient world) on the wounds. He then took the wounded man to an inn "and took care of him" (10:34). When he had to continue his journey, he brought the innkeeper into the network of care, paying him to look after the man. We are part of many interweaving networks and they need to work together to create solidarity. We need good employers, good health care, safe roads. Pope Francis says that this parable summons us "to rediscover our vocation as citizens... builders of a new social bond".[10] Everything is connected, everyone is connected. In one version of globalisation, this is little more than networks of convenience, efficiency and entertainment. In Christian thought, this is the central insight that we are all related as God's family, with a divine origin and an eternal destiny. We are therefore called to care for everyone. We are called to "direct society to the pursuit of the common good",[11] which means identifying where change needs to happen.

Pope Francis builds on the teaching of John Paul II that solidarity is a virtue, something that you do, by being more specific about what needs to be done. Solidarity, he says, "is more than engaging in sporadic acts of generosity".[12] It is a mindset that thinks in terms of community; it means that the lives of all are more important than the accumulation of goods by a few. It means, and this has not always been a major chord in Catholic Social Teaching, "combating the structural causes of poverty, inequality, the lack of work, land and housing, the denial of social and labour rights".[13] Where do we find the structural causes of poverty? We know that they are rooted in original sin, the desire to grasp and possess, but where are the manifestations? As we noted in the previous chapter, they are embedded in the culture and practice of systems, such as the benefits system, the immigration system, the prison system and employment legislation. Poverty is not an accident; it is "designed in" to systems and institutions and it can be designed out.

Pope Francis also wants us to focus on the bigger picture, the overarching system that leads to injustice and poverty, which is the current economic model. The many forms of injustice in the world are fed by a "profit-based economic model that does not hesitate to exploit, discard, and even kill human beings".[14] This liberal economic model, which has held sway for decades in the West, weakens the communal dimension of life and tears at the social fabric. Its ruthless logic puts efficiency and profit before everything else, before people, before community. We can see this in our own towns and cities where basic services like banks and post offices have been closed because they are too expensive to run, the more "efficient" model being online services, even though not everyone, especially some of the most vulnerable in society, has access to the internet. We see the increasing threat to jobs from AI (artificial intelligence) technology, which some regard as unavoidable, rather than as a choice that will lead to more unemployment. The trend here, driven by a profit-first mentality that needs to be resisted, is towards *dehumanisation*.

The profit-based model always seeks to drive down labour costs and wages and put pressure on people to be more efficient, often to their psychological and physical detriment. There are around one million people in the UK on zero-hours contracts, for whom work can dry up with no notice, leaving them at the mercy of payday loan companies or even loan sharks, because they have a poor credit rating. Those who work in the warehouses of the global delivery corporations are subject to hyper-surveillance and sanctions for "wasting" even seconds. All to feed the demands of the consumer for products that are mostly not necessary for a fulfilled life and whose production and transportation inflict damage on the natural world. This is leading us to a more anxious, fragmented and globalised world, where the pace of just-in-time delivery is frenetic and the time and space for the real presence of encounter and friendship building are diminished. It breeds a culture of competition and rivalry, a culture of individualism, which, Pope Francis says, "does not make us more free, more equal, more fraternal"[15] but more grasping, more indifferent to the needs of society's victims by the side of the road. The Gospel calls us to resist this culture and be agents of change for a better world.

Jesus never did answer the lawyer's question directly. After his parable of radical solidarity with the wounded one, he asks him the question: "Which of these three, do you think, was a neighbour to the man who fell into the hands of the robbers?" (10:36). The lawyer has no choice but to say the one who helped him, although he can't bring himself to say the word "Samaritan": he just says, "The one who showed him mercy" (10:37). Jesus agrees, and his final injunction is to "go and do likewise" (10:37). In other words, *be a neighbour*, to anybody who needs you, to everybody. The Gospel does not allow us to withdraw into a belief in categories of people we can love and those we can hate. The Gospel summons us to stretch our hearts to love everybody, including, shockingly, even our enemies. We are called to build human fraternity, build bridges, not walls; to move out of our own enclosures of comfort and protection to engage with the wounded ones, to challenge the systemic violence that reduces people to victims. The Gospel begins with compassion, but does not end there. Justice and solidarity must follow. In doing this we find ourselves, since we are made for love. In doing this we find Jesus, who is forever identified with the victim by the side of the road.

There is no solidarity without **subsidiarity**, without social participation, without people enjoying the dignity of their own voice and agency. When everything is decided from the top down, when the heart and soul are ripped out of communities, human creativity and flourishing are reduced. Subsidiarity happens in many places, but it is not always named as such. Wherever voter registration and voting increase in a poor area, there is subsidiarity; wherever people get together to form a credit union to prevent others being trapped in the cycle of exploitative interest payments, there is subsidiarity; wherever local people organise to put pressure on the major employer in the area to pay a living wage, there is subsidiarity. This most abstract sounding of the principles of Catholic Social Teaching has some very recognisable and vital embodiments. A choir, a football club, a book group, an allotment association, a walking group, warm spaces, a prayer group, a union, a citizens' assembly: all examples of subsidiarity in action, inspired by solidarity. Together, not alone.

The first major expression of the principle of subsidiarity in modern CST came from Pius XI in his 1931 encyclical, *Quadragesimo Anno*. The pope's concern at the time was the loss of the old associations and guilds caused by the destructive effects of the Industrial Revolution on patterns of work and community. He was also concerned by the rise of fascism and totalitarianism, an extreme form of collectivism which was also a threat to human dignity and the common good. With that in mind, he defined subsidiarity as follows:

> Just as it is gravely wrong to take from individuals what they can accomplish by their own initiative and industry and give it to the community, so also it is an injustice and at the same time a grave evil and disturbance of right order to assign to a greater and higher association what lesser and subordinate organizations can do. For every social activity ought of its very nature to furnish help to the members of the body social, and never destroy and absorb them.[16]

For some, this has become a rallying cry for a small-state politics. The less state, the better: the more we can organise our own destiny, including our own business interests and wealth accumulation, the more free we will be. The extreme form of this is libertarianism, which is the creed of total autonomy with minimum state interference, but also little concern for the common good. It is a creed of aggressive self-reliance, of looking after your own small circle. It is a negative version of subsidiarity. A more positive version sees the importance of the state as an enabler of the development of local associations and decision making. This is closer to the vision of Pope Francis, who sees subsidiarity working in two directions: "from top to bottom and from bottom to top".[17]

When individuals, families or local communities are not able to support themselves or achieve what they need for a dignified life, Pope Francis argues, "It is then right that the highest levels of society, such as the state, should intervene to provide the necessary resources to progress."[18] He cites the example of the coronavirus pandemic, when people found themselves in deep trouble, with health and livelihoods threatened. To respond to such a threat required the institutions of the state to work together to support communities. On the other hand, society's leaders must recognise the role played by civil society, by individuals and local associations, in the creative flourishing of people and the health of communities. A balance is required of top-down and bottom-up initiatives. The criterion for decision making is the flourishing of people in community, with a preferential consideration of those who are in various forms of poverty.

Another aspect of subsidiarity that Pope Francis strongly promotes, consistent with his focus on the preferential option for the poor, is the principle of the **participation** of the most vulnerable and disadvantaged in decisions that affect the local community and economy. "The first step", he says, "is to allow the poor to tell you how they live, what they need… Let everyone speak! And this is how the principle of subsidiarity works. We cannot leave out the participation of the people; their wisdom; the wisdom of the humbler groups cannot be set aside."[19] He is particularly concerned with the power of the large corporations engaged in extractive activities that take no account of the views or experience of local, or indigenous, people. The financial institutions are listened to more readily than the workers, the ones who generate the value in an economy. During the lockdowns, we briefly realised the value of these "key workers" and showed our appreciation with public applause. That seems a distant memory now, as they struggle for decent wages and conditions in harsh economic circumstances.

The powerful corporations and vested interests have access to the corridors of power; increasingly they *are* the corridors of power. Pope Francis encourages us to listen to the wisdom of the people when it comes to shaping a future together. This is one of his keynote themes: together, not alone. The Church itself has for the most part not exemplified participation, until very recently. The role of the laity – the vast majority of the people of God – was, in the old cliché, to *pay, pray and obey*. With the new emphasis on **synodality**, this is beginning to change. Taking seriously the insights of Vatican II that the Church is the people of God and the Holy Spirit is at work in all of them, in 2021 the Church embarked on the biggest listening exercise in human history. Every diocese in the Catholic world was invited to organise opportunities for people to be listened to and for summaries of what they said to be sent to the Vatican for discernment. This is not just a one-off exercise but, despite the scepticism of some, the beginning of a new way of being Church, a Church which implements its own teaching on subsidiarity. What difference this will make to decision making at a local level remains to be seen.

Participation, inspired by solidarity, is also about responsibility, about getting involved in the community, taking an interest in what is going on, being attentive to the impact of decisions taken at local level, working to ensure that all voices are heard. The impulse of individualism is to retreat into enclaves of self-protection, cut off from the wider community. In a meritocratic world, this can happen when people become upwardly mobile through education. They arrive in a place and only seek out "people like us", which might not be the local people, the indigenous population. The culture of the local is often looked down on by the globalised work-anywhere-with-a-laptop educated elite. This is what they couldn't wait to escape from. This is the culture of walls within a community. Solidarity, on the other hand, sees everybody as a neighbour and wants to participate, to build intermediary bodies in which we learn to live together, to respect one another, to grow as relational human beings outside the narrow confines of my group, with a preferential love for the poorest.

The building up of intermediary groups or associations, which is at the heart of the practice of subsidiarity, does come with a health warning. We need to remember what we said at the beginning about the dynamics of creating groups. When a group is formed, when "membership" is defined, it involves defining those who are not in the group. So while intermediary bodies are places where we can learn social values and grow as human beings in relationship with others, growing in skills and creativity, flourishing in an experience of communion with others, they can also be closed places where prejudice and discrimination are reinforced. Our groups and associations listed above will contribute to the common good only in as much as they resist a closed culture and aggression towards those they view as in rivalry to them. They will actively undermine the common good to the extent that they exclude others, especially those who are poor.

We have often spoken in the Church about "the poor" and what we must do to relieve their miserable conditions. This thinking has been gradually changing in recent decades, beginning with Pope Paul VI who, in *Populorum Progressio*, said that "an ever more effective world solidarity should allow all peoples to become the artisans of their destiny".[20] It is no longer a case of helping the poor by telling them what they need, but using our own resources and influence to involve those who are poor in their own development, to help to restore their dignity. Pope Francis mentions the popular movements as key players in this work. He calls them the social poets who help to make possible an integral human development "that goes beyond the idea of social policies being a policy *for* the poor, but never *with* the poor and never *of* the poor".[21] We see many of these principles at work in community organising, which a number of Catholics have been involved in, beginning with TELCO (The East London Citizens Organisation) in the 1990s. In this movement, "the poor" are not considered to be the objects of the benevolence of those who are not poor. Instead, people who are disenfranchised or in various states of poverty are the protagonists; it is their vision that shapes a better life for the community. The success of the TELCO Living Wage for London campaign is a good example of how an organised and mobilised community can challenge injustice and bring about change.

Questions for individual reflection or group discussion:

What is your understanding of solidarity now? How do you respond to the definition of solidarity as being a neighbour, which includes combating the structural causes of poverty? Where do you see causes of poverty in your community, and what might you do to combat this? What is your understanding now of subsidiarity? Whose voices in your community are unheard; who is invisible? What might be done about this? How might you organise with others to build better social bonds and living conditions in your community?

Quotations from sacred scripture and the teaching of the Church:

"Pray then in this way:
Our Father in heaven,
hallowed be your name,
Your kingdom come.
Your will be done,
on earth as it is in heaven.
Give us this day our daily bread.
And forgive us our debts,
as we also have forgiven our debtors.
And do not bring us to the time of trial,
but rescue us from the evil one."

Matthew 6:9-13

"They devoted themselves to the apostles' teaching and fellowship, to the breaking of bread and the prayers."

Acts 2:42

"On the contrary, the members of the body that seem to be weaker are indispensable."

1 Corinthians 12:22

"Thus it is that the holy synod proclaims the noble calling of humanity and the existence within it of a divine seed, and offers the human race the sincere cooperation of the church in working for that universal community of sisters and brothers which is the response to humanity's calling."

Gaudium et Spes [22]

"Let us keep in mind the principle of subsidiarity, which grants freedom to develop the capabilities present at every level of society, while also demanding a greater sense of responsibility for the common good from those who wield greater power."

Pope Francis, *Laudato Si'* [23]

"The Church will have to initiate everyone – priests, religious and laity – into this 'art of accompaniment' which teaches us to remove our sandals before the sacred ground of the other (cf. *Ex* 3:5). The pace of this accompaniment must be steady and reassuring, reflecting our closeness and our compassionate gaze which also heals, liberates and encourages growth in the Christian life."

Evangelii Gaudium [24]

"Knowledge is not to be considered as a means of material prosperity and success, but as a call to serve and to be responsible for others."

Congregation for Catholic Education,
The Catholic School [25]

The voice of the lived experience of rehabilitation

My name is Brendon Kelly and I've lived at Oakleigh Road [Bradford Supported Living Services] since June 2015.

In 2014, I had a tumour on my spine. After the operation I needed, I was told I would never walk again. I was a paraplegic. My world fell apart. I'd lost my mobility, my home and my friends. This caused me to suffer from depression and anxiety.

I then moved into Oakleigh Road. I didn't want to live there – it was not my home and I didn't know anyone. I withdrew and spent my time in my bedroom and refused to speak to everyone.

Three years later, I'm walking again. I taught myself how to walk with the support of my support staff from SJOG, (St John of God Hospitaller Services).

I'm loving life. I've made new friends, built relationships with the staff team and made Oakleigh my home. This is my poem:

You'll never walk again, the doctor once said.
That was it, life was over. I retreated to bed.

You tried and you tried to make me come round;
Your kindness was useless. I didn't want to be found.

You tirelessly tried to reach out to me,
but I didn't want you or this house, don't you see?

Then slowly but surely your kindness turned me round.
I learned to walk, make new friends, live my life.

I was found![26]

References

1. Pope Francis, *Fratelli Tutti* ("On Fraternity and Social Friendship"), 73.
2. Fratelli Tutti, 27.
3. Pope Francis, *To Heal the World: Catechesis on the pandemic* (Vatican: Libreria Editrice Vaticana, 2020), 51.
4. Pope John Paul II, *Sollicitudo Rei Socialis* ("On Social Concern"), 38.
5. *Sollicitudo Rei Socialis*, 38.
6. *Sollicitudo Rei Socialis*, 38.
7. *Sollicitudo Rei Socialis*, 39.
8. Pope Francis, *Fratelli Tutti*, 67.
9. *Fratelli Tutti*, 30.
10. *Fratelli Tutti*, 66.
11. *Fratelli Tutti*, 66.
12. *Fratelli Tutti*, 116.
13. *Fratelli Tutti*, 116.
14. *Fratelli Tutti*, 22.
15. Fratelli Tutti, 105.
16. Pope Pius XI, *Quadragesimo Anno* ("On Reconstruction of the Social Order"), 79.
17. *To Heal the World*, 78.
18. *To Heal the World*, 78.
19. *To Heal the World*, 80.
20. Pope Paul VI, *Populorum Progressio* ("On the Development of Peoples"), 65.
21. *Fratelli Tutti*, 169.
22. Second Vatican Council, *Gaudium et Spes* (Pastoral Constitution on the Church in the Modern World), 3.
23. Pope Francis, *Laudato Si'* ("On Care for Our Common Home"), 196.
24. Pope Francis, *Evangelii Gaudium* ("The Joy of the Gospel"), 169.
25. Congregation for Catholic Education, *The Catholic School*, 56.
26. St John of God Hospitaller Services, https://sjog.uk/what.php, accessed 4 June 2023.

CARE OF CREATION: TOWARDS AN INTEGRAL ECOLOGY

> ***Topics covered:*** *the roots of the climate crisis in original sin – the need for ecological conversion, a change of heart – integral ecology as being in loving relationship with God, neighbour and creation – the need for education and formation of ecological citizens – change of lifestyle – pressure on economic interests to change – the revelation of God in nature.*

"We are on a highway to climate hell with our foot still on the accelerator."[1] António Guterres, the secretary-general of the United Nations, did not hold back when he addressed the delegates at the COP27 conference in Egypt on 7 November 2022. He was sounding a dire warning that time is running out if we are to reverse the damage to our climate caused by human activity. Global warming, caused among other things by the burning of fossil fuels to feed our obsession with economic growth, is an existential threat to our garden-planet. Guterres warned that, to have any chance of limiting the global rise in temperature to 1.5 degrees Celsius, we need to achieve global net zero emissions by 2050. Net zero is when the greenhouse gases going into the atmosphere are balanced by their removal out of the atmosphere. This target is looking precarious. We are on the point of no return.

The prophetic voice of the Church has been steadily gathering confidence and clarity on the topic of climate change, beginning with Pope Paul VI in the 1970s, with increasing concern from Popes John Paul II and Benedict XVI, culminating in *Laudato Si'* by Pope Francis, the first papal encyclical to be devoted entirely to the climate crisis, published in 2015. Pope Francis does not hold back either: "The earth, our home, is beginning to look more and more like an immense pile of filth."[2] More than a third of the food we produce is wasted. Steaming landfills pile up with non-biodegradable materials. Pope Francis characterises our society as a "throwaway culture",[3] which discards not only waste but people as well, with no regard for the common good.

The pope expands the horizon of Catholic Social Teaching from the human community to the whole of creation, of which we are a part. "The climate is a common good, belonging to all and meant for all," he says. Solidarity is now understood as communion with all creatures, indeed with all material creation. He calls us "to recognise the need for changes of lifestyle, production and consumption, in order to combat this warming or at least the human causes which produce or aggravate it".[4] We cannot walk by the stricken body of our earth with nervous indifference. We are all implicated in what is happening, since "we all generate small ecological damage".[5] We all have a responsibility to act, in a spirit of global solidarity.

One of the key themes of *Laudato Si'* is that everything is connected and related. There is not an environmental crisis and a social crisis; there is one complex crisis which is social and environmental. This means that the solutions demand "an integrated approach to combating poverty, restoring dignity to the excluded, and at the same time protecting nature".[6] Let us look again at the root cause of this crisis, from a Christian perspective. In Chapter Three we noted that Pope Francis described sin as wanting to "possess and exploit that which we do not value as gift",[7] rejecting the limits that love requires. We can see the consequences of this sinful behaviour in the exploitation of the environment to feed a consumerist lifestyle. This attitude sees the earth not as a gift but as a commodity, to be plundered for our own ends.

This is the sin of Adam, the grasping by humankind that is at the root of original sin. This grasping is the basic cause of the social and environmental crisis. It is rejecting the wisdom that as human beings our freedom is not limitless. In the Christian understanding of the human person, who we are does not start with us. It starts with our Creator. We are part of his creation. Being a creature does not diminish us; our createdness is a gift from God. The right responses to a gift, when it is received *as* a gift, are gratitude and responsibility for the gift. As part of creation, God's plan was for us to "till and keep" (Genesis 2:15) the garden of the earth and to live in holiness and justice, in right relation with God, each other and nature. We rejected that balance and harmony and sought to possess what we desired for our own satisfaction, no matter what the cost to other human beings or nature.

This grasping way of life, what the pope calls "compulsive consumerism",[8] leads to anxiety and violence, since we will never have enough and never have more than the so-called success stories of this culture. Since the damage and degradation we see in the social and environmental crisis are the symptoms of a grasping heart, that's where we must look for the solution. It's not a matter of just changing our behaviour by an act of will. The Christian contribution to this crisis insists that the solution begins with no less than an "ecological conversion",[9] a change of heart. For the Christian this means that their "encounter with Jesus Christ becomes evident in their relationship with the world around them".[10] For Pope Francis, this conversion is at the heart of our Christian life, not an optional extra. As we noted in Chapter Four, the vision of Jesus for human flourishing involved a *divestment* of power and possessions, a letting go, not a grasping. In Luke's Gospel, we saw the connection between the desire to accumulate wealth and hardness of heart towards the poor (The Rich Fool, Lazarus and the Rich Man).

For the young people in our schools and parishes, who are groomed by the culture of consumption and the cult of appearance, this means there is another vision of being human. It is a call to be loving, to move from "what I want to what God's world needs".[11] It is a call to be converted to a simpler lifestyle, where less is more. It is a life that is content with encountering others, being of service to others, developing our gifts; a life of prayer, in contact with nature. It is an alternative definition of happiness from the one held out by the purveyors of the consumer culture. In this counter-cultural vision, "happiness means knowing how to limit some needs which only diminish us and being open to the many different possibilities which life can offer".[12] It is life to the full, but not the version seen on social media. The odds are stacked against this message getting through, but that should not stop us trying.

This life to the full is found in loving relationships, a going out from ourselves. **Integral ecology** defines the set of relationships involved in this fullness of life as *God-self-neighbour-nature*. It is the opposite of the me-centred culture. In the parable of the Rich Man, we see an image of a life closed in on itself and its pleasures. Before Jesus tells the parable, he explains to the crowd what it means, as if this message was too important to be lost in translation. He tells the crowd to be on guard against all kinds of greed, because "life does not consist in the abundance of possessions" (Luke 12:15). He then tells them the parable of the man who thought that the bumper harvest belonged to him, so he built bigger barns and then he threw a party – for himself, literally. He says to his soul, "Soul, you have ample goods laid up for many years; relax, eat, drink, be merry" (12:19). It is a very modern image of individualism, alienation, a person cut off from all relationships apart from with himself and his wealth.

Pope Francis holds up his namesake and inspiration, St Francis of Assisi, as the example *par excellence* of integral ecology. St Francis was "a mystic and a pilgrim who lived in simplicity and in wonderful harmony with God, and others, with nature and with himself. He shows us just how inseparable the bond is between concern for nature, justice for the poor, commitment to society and interior peace."[13] This is the cycle of life-giving relationships that constitutes human flourishing. This is what it means to be fully human. To be in right relationship means, first of all, to be in communion with God, then with our neighbour and then with all of creation. Inner peace involves knowing that we have been created by a loving God for a loving purpose; it involves living out that reality in faith. But that alone is not sufficient for life to the full. If it's all about me and God, with no concern for my neighbour or the natural world, then that is not integral, that is not life to the full.

In the Christian vision, the relationship with my neighbour is inextricably linked to my relationship with nature. The deterioration of the social fabric and the natural world, from the same root cause in greed and the urge to exploit, affects the most vulnerable people on the planet disproportionately. Water pollution, rising sea levels, loss of farming land – all have their most severe impact on the poorest people on the earth, who are then often forced to migrate from their homes, although this climate-induced migration is not recognised in international conventions as a criterion for refugee status. This is why Pope Francis insists that we need to hear "both the cry of the earth and the cry of the poor".[14] We cannot claim to believe in God without concern for our neighbours, especially the poorest, and for our environment.

At an organisational level, an example of distortion of integral ecology might be if there is a commitment to divesting (or disinvesting) in fossil fuel companies, investing in companies providing renewable energy, but not paying employees a real living wage, or committing to the mental health and well-being of the workforce. In such cases, the ecology is out of kilter. You can see this in some schools or parishes where all the energy and focus is on the climate crisis, but there is little attention to the situation in the local community and what might be done to help to restore the social fabric. It can of course work the other way, with all the focus on local need and little regard for ecological citizenship. We must learn to hear both the cry of the earth and the cry of the poor.

Since the Industrial Revolution, which began in Britain in the 1750s, we have been extracting value from the earth and our fellow human beings for the creation of wealth and goods on an enormous scale. The wealth generated by the workers has not been shared equally, with most value flowing to the owners. The low wages of the workers maximised the profits for the owners. The west end of the cities and towns of Britain are full to this day of the mansions of the industrial owning classes (upwind of the toxic plumes that swept over the east end). Those who have suffered most are the poor and the earth. This revolution, powered by the burning of fossil fuels, especially coal, has released into the atmosphere unprecedented amounts of carbon dioxide, a greenhouse gas which traps the sun's heat in the earth's atmosphere. This is the main cause of the steep increase in global warming in the last two hundred years. Its harmful effects on the environment are increasingly obvious, including "intense droughts, water scarcity, severe fires, rising sea levels, flooding, melting polar ice, catastrophic storms and declining biodiversity".[15] Our planet truly is sick.

Other significant causes of warming, such as deforestation, are also driven by the global demand for the products of a lifestyle of pleasure and consumption, such as meat and palm oil. Changing our habits of consumption – including what we eat – would lessen the demand for these products. The problem is that too many of us are more than happy with this lifestyle. It's what we aspire to; it's associated with success. Pope Francis, sounding at times like an Old Testament prophet, identifies the cause of our indifference to the fate of the planet and the plight of the poor as "a covetous heart, the feverish pursuit of pleasures, and a blunted conscience".[16] We are unmoved by the reality that in global terms we are a minority that "believes it has the right to consume in a way which can never be universalised".[17] If everyone on the planet lived as we do in the West, with our patterns of consumption, the earth could not even cope with the waste that would be generated.

A radical reappraisal is required if we are to avoid climate catastrophe. "There needs to be a distinctive way of looking at things, a way of thinking, policies, an educational programme, a lifestyle and a spirituality which together generate resistance to the assault of the technocratic paradigm."[18] We are called to resist, to say "no" to the dominant culture and propose a different way of living on the earth. This is where our schools and parishes can play such a vital role. The creation of an "ecological citizenship"[19] involves a critique of the myths of modernity, such as "individualism, unlimited progress, competition, consumerism, the unregulated market".[20] This citizenship is rooted in our spirituality; it should facilitate "making the leap to the transcendent which gives ecological ethics its deepest meaning".[21] This is what distinguishes the Christian approach to creation from others. We start with creation as God's gift and human beings as the image of God, stewards and co-creators.

We need education and formation in new habits, a new lifestyle of moderation and humility, inspired by the Gospel. This is something we have been called to from the beginning of Christianity. It has just taken on more urgency, as we live with the consequences of having turned away from this lifestyle in recent years. Even the smallest actions to live more simply have worth. It is easy to lose hope in the face of climate damage on a global scale. What difference will my small efforts make, compared to the greenhouse gas emissions from China, the United States and India? The pope encourages us to make those small efforts to live simply, to reuse and recycle, for example, because they are how we should be living as stewards of God's good earth. But we are called to go further.

In the previous chapter we made the link between solidarity and combating the structural causes of injustice. The structural causes of climate warming may seem daunting to challenge, but the pope reminds us of the success of consumer boycotts of certain products, forcing businesses to consider their environmental footprint. Our changes in lifestyle can bring "healthy pressure to bear on those who wield political, economic and social power".[22] The emphasis is on *healthy* pressure. The Gospel does not call us to violence. Any pressure we bring for change must be non-violent and consider the impact on the common good, on the most vulnerable. Catholic Social Teaching advocates action against injustice, but never confrontational or violent action. Change for the good often requires pressure to be put on those in power, who will seldom give up lightly what is to their advantage, but always with the balancing of all the principles of CST in mind. We'll look at this more closely in Chapter Ten.

The final point to stress when it comes to taking action is that it should involve the community, not just the individual. This approach builds relationships and helps to restore the social fabric that has been so badly frayed by the profit-driven era, which has no regard for the common good. Community action is also a way to "break out of the indifference induced by consumerism".[23] Not everyone will have the same role to play in activity towards justice. At St Paul reminded us, there are many gifts in the body of Christ, but everyone has a role to play in building a culture of care.

We see this care for creation from Jesus when he said, "Are not five sparrows sold for two pennies? Yet not one of them is forgotten in God's sight" (Luke 12:6). We do not care for creation only because we are so deeply interwoven with its fate, or even because it is beautiful, but because it is part of our God-given inheritance, and "each creature reflects something of God".[24] The tradition of the Church often referred to the two books that reveal God to us, the book of the word of God and the book of nature. The universe speaks to us of the love of God; in the poetic phrase of Pope Francis, the material universe is like a "caress of God".[25] St Thomas Aquinas teaches that the wonderful diversity we see in nature is willed by God so that "what was wanting to one in the representation of the divine goodness might be supplied by another".[26] We live in networks of relatedness, responsible for each other in a spirit of universal solidarity. All things exist in dependence on each other, "to complete each other, in the service of each other".[27]

St Francis of Assisi, our patron saint of integral ecology, was inspired by his Teacher, Jesus of Nazareth. Jesus, as a poor working man living in Palestine two thousand years ago, trod lightly on the earth. What we would now call his "carbon footprint" was negligible. He lived in close relationship with nature, as did all his agrarian community. They lived off the land, with little to spare, consuming what they needed. As a Jew, he was formed in the theology of his people, with a deep appreciation of creation as a gift from God. He used images from the natural world to illustrate his vision of the slow, purposeful growth of the kingdom of God, such as the mustard seed (Mark 4:30-32). His life was defined by his relationship with his Father. He knew he was "Beloved" (Luke 3:22). He often went off by himself to quiet places to pray, to be in communion with his Father (Luke 6:12). He lived to do the will of his Father. He lived for others, restoring dignity to the marginalised and oppressed. He had time for others, teaching them even when he was tired (Mark 6:34), spending long evenings with his disciples explaining the parables. He showed no interest at all in possessions or worldly power. He was, in the terms we have been using, a model, *the* model, of integral ecology: in right relationship with God, his fellow human beings and nature. His mission was to restore us in those relations, so that we might have life to the full.

God's creation is a gift, a *decision*, to make this universe out of nothing. Creation is animated by the Spirit of God. We saw that earlier when we looked at the creation accounts in Genesis. God's Spirit (Hebrew: *ruach*) hovered over the water. In the creation of man in Genesis 2, God breathed into the nostrils of Adam, giving him life with his very breath. When humankind turned its back on the original intention of God, violence spread everywhere on earth, such that God made a flood to arise and sweep all humankind away, apart from Noah and his family and the creatures in the ark. When they settled on dry land, God made a covenant with them, one of several binding promises in the Bible. What is striking about this covenant is that it is between God and every living creature. The sign of this covenant, which still stirs wonder in us even in our scientific age, is the rainbow: "When the bow is in the clouds, I will see it and remember the everlasting covenant between God and every living creature of all flesh that is on the earth" (Genesis 9:16). God will never destroy his creation by water again, and neither should we.

Questions for individual reflection or group discussion:

What is your understanding of integral ecology? Can you see it at work in your life, in the life of your community, or is it out of kilter in some respect, favouring one of the relationships over the others? What might be done to bring the relationships more into harmony?

Quotations from sacred scripture and the teaching of the Church:

> "For six years you shall sow your field, and for six years you shall prune your vineyard, and gather in their yield; but in the seventh year there shall be a sabbath of complete rest for the land."
>
> Leviticus 25:3-4

"The earth is the LORD's and all that is in it,
the world, and those who live in it;
for he has founded it on the seas,
and established it on the rivers."

Psalm 24:1-2

"Therefore I tell you, do not worry about your life, what you will eat or what you will drink, or about your body, what you will wear. Is not life more than food, and the body more than clothing? Look at the birds of the air; they neither sow nor reap nor gather into barns, and yet your heavenly Father feeds them. Are you not of more value than they?"

Matthew 6:25-26

"Ever since the creation of the world his eternal power and divine nature, invisible though they are, have been understood and seen through the things he has made."

Romans 1:20

"The dominion granted to man by the Creator is not an absolute power, nor can one speak of a freedom to 'use and misuse,' or to dispose of things as one pleases. The limitation imposed from the beginning by the Creator himself and expressed symbolically by the prohibition not to 'eat of the fruit of the tree' (cf. Gen 2:16-17) shows clearly enough that, when it comes to the natural world, we are subject not only to biological laws but also to moral ones, which cannot be violated with impunity. A true concept of development cannot ignore the use of the elements of nature, the renewability of resources and the consequences of haphazard industrialization – three considerations which alert our consciences to the moral dimension of development."

Pope John Paul II, *On Social Concern*, 34

"There is a nobility in the duty to care for creation through little daily actions, and it is wonderful how education can bring about real changes in lifestyle. Education in environmental responsibility can encourage ways of acting which directly and significantly affect the world around us, such as avoiding the use of plastic and paper, reducing water consumption, separating refuse, cooking only what can reasonably be consumed, showing care for other living beings, using public transport or car-pooling, planting trees, turning off unnecessary lights, or any number of other practices. All of these reflect a generous and worthy creativity which brings out the best in human beings. Reusing something instead of immediately discarding it, when done for the right reasons, can be an act of love which expresses our own dignity."

Pope Francis, *Laudato Si'*, 211

"The human person grows more, matures more and is sanctified more to the extent that he or she enters into relationships, going out from themselves to live in communion with God, with others and with all creatures."

Pope Francis, *Laudato Si'*, 240

References

1. António Guterres, https://www.un.org/sg/en/content/sg/speeches/2022-11-07/secretary-generals-remarks-high-level-opening-of-cop27, accessed 11 April 2023.
2. Pope Francis, *Laudato Si'* ("On Care for Our Common Home"), 21.
3. *Laudato Si'*, 22.
4. *Laudato Si'*, 23.
5. *Laudato Si'*, 8.
6. *Laudato Si'*, 139.
7. Pope Francis, *Let Us Dream* (London: Simon and Schuster, 2020), 34.
8. *Laudato Si'*, 203.
9. *Laudato Si'*, 217.
10. *Laudato Si'*, 217.
11. *Laudato Si'*, 9.
12. *Laudato Si'*, 223.
13. *Laudato Si'*, 10.
14. *Laudato Si'*, 49.
15. United Nations, *Climate Action*: https://www.un.org/en/climatechange/what-is-climate-change, accessed 13 April 2023.
16. Pope Francis, *Evangelii Gaudium* ("The Joy of the Gospel"), 2.
17. *Laudato Si'*, 50.
18. *Laudato Si'*, 111.
19. *Laudato Si'*, 211.
20. *Laudato Si'*, 210.
21. *Laudato Si'*, 210.
22. *Laudato Si'*, 206.
23. *Laudato Si'*, 232.
24. *Laudato Si'*, 221.
25. *Laudato Si'*, 84.
26. *Laudato Si'*, 86.
27. *Laudato Si'*, 86.

Integral Ecology

Option for the poor

Structures of solidarity

Wider "we"

JUSTICE

F

S

GOD

TRUTH

LOVE

HS

Common good

Universal destination of goods

Shared possessions

Image of God

Co-creators

Live simply

"The kingdom of God is justice and peace, and joy in the Holy Spirit."

Romans 14:7

THE COMMON GOOD: A VISION FOR RENEWAL

> ***Topics covered:*** *the peace of the Risen Christ as starting point for the common good – Christians as ambassadors of reconciliation, called to build a better world, to restore relationships – definition and key elements of the common good in Church teaching – the family and the common good – option for the poor at heart of the common good – the New Law of love.*

A huddled figure moves quickly through the pre-dawn gloom. She is heading to a garden outside the city of Jerusalem, where there is a tomb. Behind a heavy stone at the entrance to the tomb, in cold pitch blackness, on a ledge carved out of the rock, lies the cleaned and anointed body of Jesus, wrapped from head to foot in linen cloths. Or at least that's what Mary Magdalene expected to find; but this is no ordinary story. This is the Christian account of creation. St John in his Gospel indicates as much by saying it was the first day of the week and "still dark" (John 20:1), as it was when the Spirit of God hovered over the waters of chaos. This is Genesis II, the fulfilment of creation, in a garden, with the stone rolled away and an empty tomb. Mary runs back and tells Peter and the Beloved Disciple that the body of Jesus has been taken. They make haste to the tomb. Peter runs straight in and sees the linen cloths, but no body. The air is charged with nervous energy. First light is spreading. What in God's name is going on? The two men run back to the others, leaving Mary on her own, weeping.

She looks into the tomb again and sees two angels, like the two angels on the "mercy seat", the lid of the ark of the covenant, protecting the presence of God within (Exodus 25:18–21; 1 Samuel 4:4). But the presence is no longer there. Mary turns and sees Jesus, but doesn't recognise him. She takes him to be the gardener. "Woman, why are you weeping?" he asks her (20:15). We are back in the Garden of Eden and Mary is Eve

(Genesis 2:23). Jesus is the New Adam, with echoes of the Lord who walked in the garden in Genesis, looking for his wayward children. Jesus now calls her by name, "Mary" (20:16), and her eyes are opened; she knows her Lord. Her instinct is to cling to him: old habits of grasping die hard, even in trying to love. But Jesus must ascend to his Father. A new mode of abiding divine presence will be sent from God. She goes back to tell the disciples: she is the apostle to the apostles, as tradition calls her, the bearer of the good news of the resurrection to the Church.

That evening, the disciples are gathered in a room (the upper room of the Last Supper?) with the doors locked for fear of the religious authorities. Despite Mary's amazing news, they are still in the old world of us and them, fear and suspicion. Then the extraordinary happens. Jesus is among them, crucified and risen. His first words bear no trace of resentment at the betrayals and denials, no sense of vengeance on those who mocked him, beat him and tortured him to death. He simply says, "Peace be with you" (20:21) and shows them his wounds. This is the Lamb of God, the forgiving victim, forgiving us. This is a peace the world does not know (John 14:27). The world cannot sustain an abiding peaceful presence. There may be security for a while, only to turn into anxiety. Jesus offers the abiding peace of God. He does not stop the chaos and violence of the world, but he is present within it, in a new way, to offer a way out.

The second time he bestows peace on the disciples, it is with a mission. The life of God is not to be clung on to, it is not a private possession. It is only received and given away. He sends them forth and breathes the Holy Spirit into them, just as God breathed life into the nostrils of Adam (Genesis 2:7). They will be part of this new creation as they forgive sins, "loosing" human beings from the rivalry and violence that has bound them down. The new creation, a new humanity, will be built on forgiveness. The path to renewal is through reconciliation, letting go of the divisions, injustice and violence, building a universal communion. The Jesuit theologian Karl Rahner said, "Resurrection is the beginning of the transformation of the world."[1] Just as we were invited to till and keep the garden of the world in Genesis, so in John's Gospel we are called to be co-creators in this work of the new creation, building the common good, the conditions that allow all human beings to flourish.

In this work we begin with the poorest of the poor, the victims, the scapegoats, the ones who are sacrificed by a throwaway culture of success at all costs. This is where we will find Jesus. In the words of Pope Benedict XVI, "Christ took the lowest place in the world – the Cross – and by his radical humility he redeemed us and constantly comes to our aid".[2] Jesus is forever identified with the most vulnerable – the sick, the hungry, the naked, the prisoner – and so must Christians be. The message of the resurrection is no more victim making, no more degradation and exploitation, no more violence, no more us against them, no more separation and suspicion, no more living behind the locked doors of fear and anxiety. The Spirit of God is peace and forgiveness for those whose hearts are open to this new life. This mission of God, of which Christians are ambassadors, is to transform relationships in the world, promote peace and reconciliation and restore dignity with compassion and justice, beginning with the weakest and poorest:

> Church communities, brought together by the message of Jesus Christ and gathered in the Holy Spirit around the Risen Lord, offer themselves as places of communion, witness and mission, and as catalysts for the redemption and transformation of social relationships.[3]

This seems like a good place to start when considering the common good. For some, the starting point is heaven, the Beatific Vision, our communion with God, our destiny, and we work backwards from that to think what it begins to look like in this life. This approach makes good sense, but what about also working forward from that moment in the upper room when the risen Jesus breathed the Holy Spirit into the disciples and sent them out as ambassadors of reconciliation? What does the world look like when it begins to be changed by the Spirit of the Risen Christ, when the dignity of every person is restored and there is no more exclusion or poverty? The principle of the common good, the *Compendium* tells us, "stems from the dignity, unity and equality of all people".[4]

Ambassadors of this great project, which we also call the reign of God, have a key requirement. The entry into this role of ambassador is *conversion of the heart*, of being open to receiving this forgiveness in faith, which is imparted by baptism. It is part of the mystery of our dignity as human beings that we can always harden our hearts to this new life. But there is a way out of this enclosure in ourselves: "Jesus Christ came in order to bring us out of our imprisonment in sin. Creation, which had become entangled in sin, is liberated by Christ for love and justice. The 'civilisation of love' begins with the conversion of the individual and his or her reconciliation with God."[5]

It is a spiritual revolution. St Paul calls Christians to be "renewed in the spirit of your minds" (Ephesians 4:23), to put away the former way of life, corrupt and deluded, and put on a "new self, created according to the likeness of God in true righteousness [justice] and holiness" (4:24). It sounds as if the children of the new creation are back in the garden, in that state of original justice and holiness. At least, that's the possibility that has now opened up. We are called to be transformed, to be new selves in the image of God, who will live in right relationship with God, each other and the earth.

The common good is a vision of a restored and reconciled humanity, no longer blighted by injustice. The common good is, if you like, the master concept of Catholic Social Teaching; it's what we're aiming for, in this life. When the dignity of the person is recognised and upheld, when there is genuine solidarity between people, a sense of kinship and community, when that community is served by co-operative and creative associations open to all, when the state works to ensure that the goods necessary for a decent life are fairly distributed, then we are beginning to see the common good become a reality.

In modern political terms, the common good is often used as a term for what is good for the majority of people. This is utilitarianism, not the common good. In the Catholic tradition the common good is the good of all and of the whole person. The most authoritative definition is found in Vatican II's *Gaudium et Spes*, which states that the common good can be understood as "the sum total of social conditions which allow people, either as groups or as individuals, to reach their fulfilment more fully and more easily".[6] The *Catechism* goes on to outline the three essential elements of the common good. The first is "respect for the person".[7] Public authorities are called to respect the fundamental rights of the human person, which include the right to act according to conscience, in a society that allows the human person to fulfil their vocation, to flourish as the human beings God intended them to be in relationships with others.

The second element is "social well-being and development".[8] Civil authorities have a role to play in arbitrating between the interests and needs of different groups, but they also have a duty to make accessible "what is needed to lead a truly human life",[9] which includes food, clothing, health, work, education and culture. This is rooted in the principle of the universal destination of goods, which we first encountered back in Chapter Two; the principle that "God has destined the earth and all it contains for the use of everyone and of all peoples, so that the good things of creation should be available equally to all".[10] When people do not have enough to eat, or the resources to keep themselves warm, as we have seen in the UK during the cost-of-living crisis and long before that, it is a failure of the common good, a failure to distribute the goods of the earth in a just way. As the Fathers of the early Church often said, when we give to those who are poor, we are only giving to them what is their due. Pope Francis quotes St John Chrysostom, who puts it this way: "Not to share our wealth with the poor is to rob them and take away their livelihood. The riches we possess are not our own, but theirs as well."[11]

The third essential element for the common good is peace; that is, "the stability and security of a just order".[12] In the tradition of Catholic Social Teaching, it is the role of the state to promote and defend the common good of civil society and its citizens. By morally acceptable means, the state should ensure the security of society. Not by oppression and coercion, but by a morally accountable security apparatus and an impartial judiciary. There is no peace without justice, so this peace cannot simply be an imposition by unjust structures, which leads to further injustice. Beyond the borders of the state, we also need to consider the unity of the human family, all equal in natural dignity, in other words a "universal common good",[13] a concept which Pope Paul VI addressed so compellingly in *Populorum Progressio* (see Chapter Five).

The responsibility for peace is not just the responsibility of the state, but also of the human person, of all of us. We are called by the Gospel to be peacemakers and peace-bearers in our own communities, especially in the family. In the Catholic tradition, the family is "the first and vital cell of society".[14] It is, in the wonderful phrase of Pope John Paul II, "the cradle of life and love".[15] In this cradle the human person grows and learns from his or her parents, our first educators. In this setting, loved by their parents, children become aware of their dignity, are formed in values and are prepared for life in society with their unique set of qualities and gifts, with a capacity for healthy relationship and creativity.

The family is the first community we experience as human beings. We cannot find fulfilment in ourselves; we are made to be in communion, in community. That is why the cult of individualism is so damaging. It is a distortion of the way we were made. We can only find our true identity "with" and "for" others. The family is a school of formation for the common good.

We know, however, that families can also be places of harm where children do not flourish. In some families too, the relationship between husband and wife can be destroyed by abusive and controlling behaviour. During the COVID-19 lockdown, there was a significant increase in domestic abuse, mostly against women, although some men are also victims of domestic violence. Anyone who works in a school setting knows that so many of the challenges young people face in school can be traced back to circumstances at home. We can no longer take for granted that our young people know how to form healthy and loving relationships. As we noted in Chapter Six, misogyny is rife in social media and in our institutions. Restoring healthy relationships to couples, guiding young people in the basics of healthy relationships, is an increasingly urgent work of the common good. In Part II, there's a spotlight on Safe in Faith, a remarkable charity in Westminster Diocese that works to restore hope and dignity to victims of domestic abuse and to train clergy to deal with disclosures of abuse in sensitive and helpful ways. In Part III, you'll find a link to the website of the charity Marriage Care, which provides preparation for healthy couple relationships and support for when they're not healthy.

To briefly recap, then: the common good is the good of all people in society and the whole person. It is the conditions required for living a truly human life, which are the material conditions as well as cultural and spiritual conditions. The Church is a promoter and defender of the human person in all their dimensions. The first building block of the common good is the family, where the person is formed in values with a sense of dignity, the importance of loving relationships over time, and an understanding of the value of community. The state should support the common good and the family especially. Other intermediate bodies are also necessary for the common good, for the growth and flourishing of human beings. This is what's known in CST as subsidiarity, as we saw in Chapter Seven. It's in these intermediate associations, when they are not closed in on themselves and defined by prejudice, that we learn about life beyond the family, how to participate well in society and how to encounter people with very different needs and outlooks from ours. The very concept of the common good, with community at its heart, is at odds with the dominant ideology of today's culture, which is the cult of the autonomous individual.

The principle of the common good is not about trying to ensure that we all agree with each other, but about a disposition that we are all in this together; we are working towards a communion of people in which we enjoy a sense of belonging and safety, in which we have an opportunity to live fully human lives. This means that we need to disagree well, without descending into violence and discord. This means that we must be attentive to wherever life is not flourishing. If it is not the common good for one person, it is not the common good of all. In a proactive and reactive way, we must work for the good of all. We are reactive to whatever legislation is proposed at national or local levels, with particular attention to the impact on the most vulnerable, not just the impact on me, or my family, or my club. We are proactive as we consider together creative projects that build community and participation. We can also be proactive in helping to shape laws that are in the legislative pipeline, or bringing forward creative suggestions to enhance the common good.

The overarching narrative we have touched on at various points already is that in the last few decades, certainly since the Second

World War, our society has lost what we used to call the social virtues, the sense of solidarity that comes from living in community. We have become a more individualistic society, obsessed with having, not being, consuming, not creating. We have become a society of contract, not covenant. A contract is an exchange of goods for mutual benefit. I give, I get. The older language of covenant is based on trust, commitment and loyalty. Marriage is an example of a covenant (although for some it is also a contract), a life entered into by two people for better or worse, until death. It is a promise, an act of faith, a desire to do together what neither could do alone. It creates community. It is a place where people can grow in love and friendship. Our society is a community of such communities. It is in society that we can build bonds of co-operation, not competition.

In *Fratelli Tutti*, Pope Francis reflects on the damage that has been done to the social fabric by decades of an economic approach driven by profit and gain, which treats workers as economic units, the rest of society as consumers, and the natural environment as a resource to be plundered at will. This can work for a while, as it did in the West after the war, as long as most people feel that their lives are improving. When the economy shrinks, as it will, then the politics of populism and anger rises up and looks for scapegoats and creates division, proposing more aggressive ways to return to prosperity, but not for all. As an antidote, Pope Francis offers social dialogue as the basis for a new culture, beyond the division and polarisation of the politics of anger, since "lack of dialogue means that… people are concerned not for the common good, but for the benefits of power".[16]

The pope calls for a culture of encounter to transcend differences and division, a recognition of our solidarity as human beings. What does a culture of encounter look like? We all have a memory of, a nostalgia for, those moments when fellowship and togetherness surfaced, maybe at a good party, a sports event, a liturgy, a moment on our doorstep banging a saucepan with everybody else in the community, in gratitude for the key workers who kept our country running during the COVID-19 lockdowns. A culture of encounter means "that we, as a people, should be passionate about meeting others, seeking points of contact, building bridges, planning a project that includes everyone. This becomes an aspiration and a style of life."[17]

Pope Francis, in his social teaching, has strongly emphasised two dimensions of the common good, which are interrelated: the preferential option for the poor and the environment. He draws our attention to what he often calls the peripheries, to those furthest away from human thriving, to those excluded from decision making and influence, to those discriminated against because they are trapped in poverty. No work of the common good is complete unless those on the peripheries are involved, indeed are protagonists, since "each of us can learn something from others. No one is useless and no one is expendable. This also means finding ways to include those on the peripheries of life. For they have another way of looking at things; they see aspects of reality that are invisible to the centres of power where weighty decisions are made."[18]

Nor is the common good served by projects or decisions that harm our natural environment. The climate is a common good; water and air and soil are common goods. Integral ecology insists on the circuit of right relations between ourselves, God, neighbour and all of creation. The common good is served when we live in greater justice and peace with one another, which includes not hoarding more than our fair share of the goods of the earth, not retreating behind the walls of our affluence. It includes intentional practices that do no harm to the environment and restore the damage we have done. It includes pursuing the inner peace of knowing that we are God's children, called to be part of a new creation. It includes befriending and walking alongside those we might not normally consider to be "one of us". It includes growing out of the mindset, however unspoken it usually is, of "one of us". Encounter is more than just occasional events that make us feel better. In the teaching of Pope Francis, it requires accompaniment, an integral part of a vision for the Church's renewal:

> The Church will have to initiate everyone – priests, religious and laity – into this "art of accompaniment" which teaches us to remove our sandals before the sacred ground of the other (cf. *Ex* 3:5). The pace of this accompaniment must be steady and reassuring, reflecting our closeness and our compassionate gaze which also heals, liberates and encourages growth in the Christian life.[19]

The common good is inspired by the Risen Christ. It is the "Law of the Gospel",[20] which is "the grace of the Holy Spirit given to the faithful through faith in Christ. It works through charity; it uses the Sermon on the Mount to teach us what must be done and makes use of the sacraments to give us the grace to do it."[21] It is the grace of the Holy Spirit breathed into the disciples in the upper room, the grace of forgiveness and peace. The New Law is not about a whole new set of external religious practices but "proceeds to reform the heart, the root of human acts... where faith, hope and charity are formed and with them the other virtues".[22] At the heart of the New Law is the "new commandment" of Jesus to his disciples: "Just as I have loved you, you also should love one another" (John 13:34). This does not just mean love one another as well as you can, but love one another "as I have loved you". This is a radical, self-emptying love, which knows no boundaries but includes love of enemies.

The Sermon on the Mount (Matthew 5:1-12) gives us a memorable portrait of the disciples of Jesus who have been transformed by this Spirit: they are poor in spirit, humble, knowing their need for

God; they mourn, because they have a heart open to the tragedy of the world; they are meek, not aggressive; they have a hunger for justice; they are pure in heart, unclouded by rivalry and the desire for possessions; they are peacemakers, not troublemakers; they are persecuted because they challenge the ways and wiles of the powerful ones. Their mission is to usher in the new creation, the kingdom of God, the common good of all. The justice that love demands is their purpose and driving force. Precisely what that justice entails and how it can be achieved in the circumstances of each moment in history is the work of prayerful discernment, which is what we turn our attention to next.

Common Good questions for individual reflection or group discussion:

Do our reflections begin in contemplative silence, making room for the Spirit of God to speak to us?

Are we primarily inward-looking or outward-facing as a community?

Do we see our "assets" – buildings, facilities, people, financial reserves – as a resource for the common good or just for our community?

Who do we not know in our community? How could we build bridges by reaching out to people or groups we have never engaged with?

Where is the decision-making power in our community? Who is included in that; who is excluded?

How can we work together to build a community in which everybody has the chance of a dignified life? Where is dignity most undermined in our community?

How can we begin to discover our own "blind spots" and prejudices in how we see what is around us?

What might a "social covenant" look like in our community; what bonds of trust and loyalty might we build in common projects and common good practices?

Quotations from sacred scripture and the teaching of the Church:

"Your ancient ruins shall be rebuilt;
You shall raise up the foundations of many generations;
You shall be called the repairer of the breach,
The restorer of streets to live in."

Isaiah 58:12

"Seek the welfare of the city where I have sent you into exile, and pray to the LORD on its behalf, for in its welfare you will find your welfare."

Jeremiah 29:7

"So if anyone is in Christ, there is a new creation: everything old has passed away; see, everything has become new! All this is from God, who reconciled us to himself through Christ, and has given us the ministry of reconciliation; that is, in Christ God was reconciling the world to himself, not counting their trespasses against them, and entrusting the message of reconciliation to us. So we are ambassadors for Christ, since God is making his appeal through us; we entreat you on behalf of Christ, be reconciled to God."

2 Corinthians 5:17-20

"To each, therefore, must be given his own share of goods, and the distribution of created goods, which, as every discerning person knows, is labouring today under the gravest evils due to the huge disparity between the few exceedingly rich and the unnumbered propertyless, must be effectively called back to and brought into conformity with the norms of the common good, that is, social justice."

Pope Pius XI[23]

"We must include the task of establishing new relationships in human society, under the mastery and guidance of truth, justice, charity and freedom – relations between individual citizens, between citizens and their respective States, between States, and finally between individuals, families, intermediate associations and States on the one hand, and the world community on the other."

Pope John XXIII[24]

"This social order requires constant improvement. It must be founded on truth, built on justice and animated by love; in freedom it should grow every day toward a more humane balance. An improvement in attitudes and abundant changes in society will have to take place if these objectives are to be gained."

Gaudium et Spes[25]

"Another important consideration is the common good. To love someone is to desire that person's good and to take effective steps to secure it. Besides the good of the individual, there is a good that is linked to living in society: the common good. It is the good of 'all of us', made up of individuals, families and intermediate groups who together constitute society. It is a good that is sought not for its own sake, but for the people who belong to the social community and who can only really and effectively pursue their good within it. To desire the *common good* and strive towards it *is a requirement of justice and charity.*"

Pope Benedict XVI[26]

"In the present condition of global society, where injustices abound and growing numbers of people are deprived of basic human rights and considered expendable, the principle of the common good immediately becomes, logically and inevitably, a summons to solidarity and a preferential option for the poorest of our brothers and sisters. This option entails recognizing the implications of the universal destination of the world's goods."

Pope Francis[27]

"Sunday is the day of the Resurrection, the 'first day' of the new creation, whose first fruits are the Lord's risen humanity, the pledge of the final transfiguration of all created reality. It also proclaims 'man's eternal rest in God'. In this way, Christian spirituality incorporates the value of relaxation and festivity."

Pope Francis[28]

"Yet we Christians are very much aware that 'if the music of the Gospel ceases to resonate in our very being, we will lose the joy born of compassion, the tender love born of trust, the capacity for reconciliation that has its source in our knowledge that we have been forgiven and sent forth. If the music of the Gospel ceases to sound in our homes, our public squares, our workplaces, our political and financial life, then we will no longer hear the strains that challenge us to defend the dignity of every man and woman'. Others drink from other sources. For us the wellspring of human dignity and fraternity is in the Gospel of Jesus Christ. From it, there arises, 'for Christian thought and for the action of the Church, the primacy given to relationship, to the encounter with the sacred mystery of the other, to universal communion with the entire human family, as a vocation of all'."

Pope Francis[29]

"We urge the Catholic people of England and Wales to take up the challenge of applying to our society all the principles of Catholic Social Teaching that we have outlined, and thus to advance the common good in collaboration with likeminded citizens of every political and religious allegiance."

Catholic Bishops' Conference of England and Wales[30]

"Men and women who are made 'new' by the love of God are able to change the rules and the quality of relationships, transforming even social structures. They are people capable of bringing peace where there is conflict, of building and nurturing fraternal relationships where there is hatred, of seeking justice where there prevails the exploitation of human beings by others. Only love is capable of radically transforming the relationships that men and women maintain among themselves."

Compendium of the Social Doctrine of the Church[31]

References

1. Karl Rahner, quoted by Dermot A. Lane, *Nature Praising God* (Dublin: Messenger Publications, 2022), 98.
2. Pope Benedict XVI, *Deus Caritas Est* ("On Christian Love"), 35.
3. *Compendium of the Social Doctrine of the Church* (London: Bloomsbury, 2004), 52.
4. Compendium, 164.
5. DOCAT, 51.
6. Second Vatican Council, *Gaudium et Spes* (Pastoral Constitution on the Church in the Modern World), 26.
7. *Catechism of the Catholic Church*, 1907.
8. *CCC*, 1908.
9. *CCC*, 1908.
10. *Gaudium et Spes*, 69.
11. Pope Francis, *Fratelli Tutti* ("On Fraternity and Social Friendship"), 119.
12. *CCC*, 1909.
13. *CCC*, 1911.
14. Second Vatican Council, *Apostolicam Actuositatem* (Decree on the Apostolate of the Laity), 11.
15. Pope John Paul II, *Christifideles Laici* ("On the Vocation and the Mission of the Lay Faithful in the Church and in the World"), 40.

16. *Fratelli Tutti*, 202.
17. *Fratelli Tutti*, 216.
18. *Fratelli Tutti*, 215.
19. Pope Francis, *Evangelii Gaudium* ("The Joy of the Gospel"), 169.
20. *CCC*, 1965.
21. *CCC*, 1966.
22. *CCC*, 1968.
23. Pope Pius XI, *Quadragesimo Anno* ("On Reconstruction of the Social Order"), 50.
24. Pope John XXIII, *Pacem in Terris* ("On Establishing Universal Peace in Truth, Justice, Charity and Liberty"), 163.
25. *Gaudium et Spes*, 26.
26. Pope Benedict XVI, *Caritas in Veritate* ("On Integral Human Development in Charity and Truth"), 7.
27. Pope Francis, *Laudato Si'* ("On Care for Our Common Home"), 158.
28. *Laudato Si'*, 237.
29. *Fratelli Tutti*, 277.
30. Catholic Bishops' Conference of England and Wales, *The Common Good*, 25.
31. *The Compendium of the Social Doctrine of the Church* (London: Bloomsbury, 2004), 4.

SEE-JUDGE-ACT: THE STEPS TO RENEWAL

> ***Topics covered:*** *the See-Judge-Act method – an example from scripture – the call to action – how can we achieve justice? – the link between See-Judge-Act and virtue.*

In St Mark's Gospel, there's a curious, quiet moment in between two scenes of high drama towards the end of the life of Jesus. First there's the triumphal entry into Jerusalem, with crowds waving palms and singing hosanna, followed the next day by the driving out of the money changers from the Temple. Two very charged scenes, for different reasons. In between, with the cries of hosanna fading in the dusk, Jesus went into the Temple. The compound was the largest in area in the ancient world. The Temple buildings were magnificent. It was the cultic heart of Judaism, the holiest place on earth, where the people came to make animal sacrifices to atone for their sins. It is now evening and quiet, we assume. The verse simply says, "Then he entered Jerusalem and went into the temple; and when he had looked around at everything, as it was already late, he went out to Bethany with the twelve" (Mark 11:11).

That's it. Nothing happens. It's an odd moment. Just when the people were expecting their messiah to come riding in from the desert and restore Israel's independence, sweeping the Romans into the sea... Jesus has a look around the Temple and then retires to his digs for the evening. What is going on here? Well, firstly, I think that is exactly the question Jesus is asking himself. He gives himself time and space to reflect. He does not get caught up in the crowd's expectations of who he is or what he should do. He goes to the Temple in the evening to escape the contagion of the crowd dynamic, to remind himself perhaps of his mission, the kind of messiah he is and the kind of kingdom he has come to announce. He has a good long look. He doesn't just glance around and make a few awestruck comments about the buildings, as the disciples do later (Mark 13:1). The sense being conveyed is that he observed closely. Jesus looks deeply into things. Like his mother, he ponders. Then he went back to Bethany with the twelve. We don't know what they talked about that evening, but I don't think it's unreasonable to imagine that Jesus might have shared what he was thinking about and what he might do next. Did they discern together what to do?

The next day he goes back to the Temple, but now he's in action mode. He drives out "those who were selling and those who were buying in the temple, and he overturned the tables of the money changers" (Mark 11:15). This was a high-profile, high-risk action, a direct assault on the heart of the Jewish religious establishment, right under the noses of the Roman army, who maintained a fortress overlooking the Temple compound. The one thing the Romans did not like was public disorder. Why does Jesus do this? What upsets him seems to be the corruption and exploitation that's going on. People bought animals for sacrifice from the Temple authorities. It was a highly lucrative business. Jesus upbraids them, saying they have turned the Temple into "a den of robbers" (Mark 11:17).

Mark tells us that the authorities were afraid of Jesus, "because the whole crowd was spellbound by his teaching" (Mark 11:18). They wanted to kill him. This was too much; this was a direct threat to their system, their hold over the people. In this account of the "cleansing of the Temple", Jesus took his time before he turned the tables over. There was observation, retreat and reflection before action. Jesus modelled what has come to be known as the **See-Judge-Act** method for applying the principles of the social doctrine of the Church. He looked around at the situation. Then he retired to reflect with his disciples. Then he acted, with no regard for his own safety. He must have known this action would set him on a collision course with the authorities, but he could not be silent in the face of corruption and the degradation of the Temple. Prophets will be persecuted because they speak out against the dominant powers and their structures of injustice.

In the Catholic Social Teaching tradition, the See-Judge-Act method was enshrined in the Magisterium (official teaching of the Church), by Pope John XXIII in his 1961 social encyclical, *Mater et Magistra*. There he states:

> There are three stages which should normally be followed in the reduction of social principles into practice. First, one reviews the concrete situation; secondly, one forms a judgment on it in the light of these same principles; thirdly, one decides what in the circumstances can and should be done to implement these principles. These are the three stages that are usually expressed in the three terms: look, judge, act.[1]

Before we look at how this approach might work in more detail, it is worth going back a step to consider what sort of action is appropriate for a follower of Jesus. The works of mercy have always been a feature of the Church. The teaching of Jesus that in feeding the hungry, welcoming the stranger, taking care of the sick and visiting those in prison, we were encountering him (Matthew 25:40), has inspired Christians through the ages and all over the world to establish places of hospitality, healing, hope and restoration. We have said already that the Gospel begins in compassion, but it does not end there. Justice must follow.

The Vatican II document *Gaudium et Spes*, the highest level of the Magisterium of Church, states that "since it has been founded on the love of the Redeemer, the church's contribution is to increase the spread of justice and charity, within nations and between nations".[2] Not just charity (love), but justice as well, right relations in society, where people receive what is their due. Pope Paul VI reinforces this point in his 1967 social encyclical *Populorum Progressio* when he says, "Lay people must consider it their task to improve the temporal order."[3] He goes on to encourage the laity not to wait for instructions from the hierarchy, but effectively to get on with it: "... the laity have the duty of using their own initiative and taking action... without waiting passively for directives and precepts from others".[4] There is a tone of urgency in his writing. Having seen for himself the scale of injustice and inequality on his world travels, he wanted Christians to respond: "Changes must be made; present conditions must be improved. And the transformations must be permeated with the spirit of the Gospel."[5]

The bishops of England and Wales, with the same sense of urgency, stated that "all Catholic citizens need an informed 'social conscience' that will enable them to identify and resist structures of injustice in their own society".[6] Identify and resist; in other words, see where the structures of injustice in society are and call them out, resist, proclaim that this is not OK; this is not God's way. And it's not enough just to talk about it, even in a public and prophetic way. Paul VI tells us that "these words will lack real weight unless they are accompanied for each individual by a livelier awareness of personal responsibility and by effective action".[7] He reminds us (you can read the full quotation at the end of the chapter) that this work of justice must come from personal conversion. It is the ongoing work of Christ's redemption, in the Church, for the world.

There can be little doubt, I hope, that the vocation of the Christian in the world is to work for justice, with compassion. What we must consider now is how to go about this work. Where do we start? What do we "see" first? We could look at the big picture of world trends: what is going on at scale? Pope Francis encourages us not to be self-referential all the time, but to look to other disciplines and authors for data and insights. C. Otto Scharmer, for example, uses three numbers to give us a vivid sense of what is going on: **1.5, 8, 800,000**. These three numbers represent what he calls the three major divides: the ecological divide, the social divide and the spiritual divide. The ecological divide can be summed up by the number 1.5. Currently our economy consumes the resources of 1.5 planets; in other words, "we use 1.5 times the regeneration capacity of planet earth".[8] That's the global average; in the United States, current consumption has surpassed five planets. You'll also remember that limiting the earth's warming to 1.5 degrees Celsius is the target to prevent irreversible harm to the environment.

The social divide can be summed up by the number 8, which is the number of billionaires who own as much as half of humankind combined: "a small group of people that can fit into a minivan owns more than the 'bottom half' of the world's population: 3.8 billion people."[9] Inequality undermines the common good. As some sections of the population become more wealthy, they have less interest in the "common goods" that benefit everybody. They will purchase private education for their children and private health care, and use their two or three cars, not public transport. This has the effect of running down public services, especially if the politicians are among the affluent. The spiritual divide can be summed up by 800,000: that's the number of people each year who die by suicide, "a number that is greater than the sum of people who are killed by war, murder and natural disasters combined".[10] Every forty seconds someone dies by suicide.

Scharmer characterises these divides as the loss of nature, the loss of society and the loss of self. In the nineteenth century, many countries saw the social divide as a major issue, as did the Church, with the publication of *Rerum Novarum* in 1891. In the last third of the twentieth century we saw the rise of the ecological divide, to which the Church responded in various papal statements, culminating in *Laudato Si'*, published in 2015. At the beginning of the twenty-first century, we see the spiritual divide, with a crisis of mental health, meaning and purpose. Scharmer estimates that advances in technology (AI) will replace about half of our jobs by 2050. "We are now facing a future", he says, "that no longer needs us."[11] This raises profound existential questions about the value of work, who we are as human beings, what kind of society we want to live in and create. After the tyrannies of the twentieth century, we are now witnessing the tyranny of technology.

We are living in a time, says Scharmer, when our planet, our societal whole and the essence of our humanity are under attack. His framing of the issue is not religious, but nevertheless he asks, where is the hope? For him, the hope is that more people, especially young people, recognise that the three divides are not three separate problems, but one problem, with the same root cause. That cause is what he calls our blind spot, which is "our inner place – the source – from which we operate when we act, communicate, perceive, or think".[12] We have lost touch with the source from which we operate. This has very close resonances with the scheme of integral ecology we outlined in Chapter Eight. In those terms, Scharmer is describing a break in the circuit of life-giving relationships between ourselves, the God who made us, our neighbour and the earth, our common home. We can see the dire consequences of this rupture all around us in 1.5, 8 and 800,000.

Can the Church offer any hope to humankind in the face of this doomsday scenario? We can and we must: that is our mission, to serve the world, to get alongside our sisters and brothers in solidarity. The three numbers of the great divides may seem too daunting for us to do anything about, but we can see their effects at the most local level. We can see inequality and poverty in our communities, the effects of global warming in our record-breaking heatwaves, the tragic effects of our spiritual crisis in the deteriorating mental health of so many, especially the young. The Church is called to do whatever it can in its local place to work for justice and human flourishing, to close those divides, to restore the life-giving circuit of relationships. Let us look now in more detail at the method to be used in this work of renewal. For this section, I have referred to the See-Judge Act framework in the Caritas Europa Grassroots Participation Programme, which can be found at: https://grassroots.caritas.eu/see-judge-act.

SEE

The first step for any group engaged in this process is to "see" the lived reality of individuals and communities around them as clearly as possible. As we said in Chapter One, this is an inductive, bottom-up approach. That means seeing, hearing and experiencing the reality in our community. This is not a desktop exercise. It could mean members of the parish or charity going out in twos, walking around the community and, like Jesus, observing closely what is going on, talking to people, gathering the stories, the data. It means naming what is happening that is a cause for concern, asking what the people in this situation are doing, feeling and saying. What is going on with the people, especially the most marginalised and disadvantaged? How do they see things? What have they got to say? *Who* are they – do we have any idea? It's important to approach this as the Good Samaritan approached the wounded man on the side of the road: we need to "draw near" to people, to allow ourselves to be moved, affected by what is going on. What stirs within us when we see the picture as fully as we can?

We could approach this on a community-wide level, trying to see the broad picture of where human life is not going well, and also where there are signs of hope, or responses already happening that we could work with. Once we've done this, we might focus in on one issue that we consider to be defining for our community, which could be the way asylum seekers are housed and made to feel welcome (or not); it could be the level of material deprivation and the high use of food banks; the number of elderly people living on their own or unvisited in care homes; it could be the alienation and frustration of young people, the level of violence, or the lack of safety on the local streets. Whatever we "see", we must be as attentive as possible to *how* we see, to see through our seeing, if you like. We see "through a glass, darkly" (1 Corinthians 13:12, KJV), as St Paul said. Our vision is partial, clouded by the effects of original sin. Where are our blind spots, our prejudices, our assumptions? The lifelong project of the Christian life is to see more like Jesus; as Pope Benedict XVI said, "The Christian's programme – the programme of the Good Samaritan, the programme of Jesus – is 'a heart which sees'. This heart sees where love is needed and acts accordingly."[13] The route to this kind of seeing is through a heart open to God's grace.

DISCERN

The next step is to judge what we have seen, but not in a punitive sense; rather, to analyse the situation and make an informed judgement about it. Some people have moved away from the term "judge" as it is now normally used negatively, and prefer to use "discern", or "think". I prefer "discern", since what we are doing next is discerning what we have seen in the light of the Gospel. There are two stages to this: social analysis and theological reflection.

Social analysis has two overriding questions: why does this situation exist and what are the root causes? These questions can be further broken down into the following:

Economic factors
Who are the owners? Who controls? Who benefits? Who pays? Who gives, who gets? What is given value? Why?

Political factors
Who decides? For whom do they decide? How do decisions get made? Who is left out of the process? What are the pathways to influence the political process?

Social factors
Who is left out? Who is included? Where is the power in any relationship? Why?

Historical factors
What past events influence the situation today?

Cultural factors
What values are evident? What do people believe in? Who influences what people believe? What cultures are celebrated and promoted?

Social analysis, which takes time and a commitment to evidence gathering and reflection, assists us in pinpointing the "heart of the matter", which then informs the theological reflection, or discernment.

Theological reflection
This part of the process is when we consider everything we have seen and learned through the lens of sacred scripture and the teaching of the Church, especially Catholic Social Teaching. For guidance on this second step, we can turn to Pope Francis who, in *Let Us Dream*, a book-length interview with Austen Ivereigh, set out in some depth and detail what was involved in the process:

> For this second step, we need not just openness to reality but a robust set of criteria to guide us: knowing we are loved by God, called to be a people in service and solidarity. We need, too, a healthy capacity for silent reflection, places of refuge from the tyranny of the urgent. Most of all we need prayer, to hear the prompts of the Spirit and cultivate dialogue in a community that can hold us and allow us to dream. Thus armed, we can read the signs of the times and opt for a way that does us all good.[14]

What Pope Francis emphasises here is the communal and spiritual nature of the reflection. We need time, space and prayer for this process. We are so schooled in the urgency of technical solutions, no-nonsense meetings that insist on outcomes, but that is not the culture of discernment. We need to resist what the pope calls the tyranny of the urgent. We need to be attuned to the prompts of the Spirit. The criteria for our discernment are the Gospel and Catholic Social Teaching: all the principles we have covered in previous chapters. He summarises the whole approach of CST as "expressions of love, that is they seek to set in motion dynamics that allow people to feel loved, especially the poor, who are able to experience their true value".[15] He urges us to begin our deliberations with the preferential option for the poor, to keep in mind how any decision might affect those who are poor. This means more than *imagining* the impact of any decision on the poorest: it means that they are in the room, involved in the process; their voices and perspectives are heard. This is skilled and sensitive work. For many communities, not used to this level of inclusion, this will be a challenge, perhaps the greatest challenge in the whole process, but perhaps the key challenge to take up.

Discernment means that you don't begin with the answer. We don't begin with a set of abstract principles and then apply them to what we have discovered. The inductive approach is the other way round. We begin with the concrete reality, as fully and deeply as we can see it, and then discern what is of God and what is not of God; what approach would humanise and what would dehumanise. Where is there good news already that we can work with? There is a kind of humility about CST, which surprises those who think of the Church as rigid and dogmatic. CST offers a way of reading reality in the light of the Gospel, which will help us to discern solutions for the injustice in our world. It's not a set of doctrinal absolutes. Pope Francis says that he has an "allergy to moralisms and other -isms that try to resolve all problems with prescriptions, equations, and rules".[16] Truth is not something we possess, but rather something we are possessed by.

When the pope talks about the "discernment of spirits", he says that the voice of God never imposes, but proposes. Even when the voice of God corrects us, it is "gently, always encouraging, consoling, giving us hope".[17] What he calls the bad spirit, on the other hand, is "strident, insistent, even monotonous… offers us dazzling solutions and tempting sensations, but they are fleeting".[18] In our discernment, it helps to know where the various voices are coming from. A strident, insistent voice that is sure of the solution, that begins with the answer based on some abstract principle, is unlikely to be from God. We hold our different options before the Lord. We pray and wait for the passages of scripture that come to prompt us; we consider the principles of Catholic Social Teaching working together, beginning with the dignity of the most marginalised. We consider the reasons for and against any course of action, trusting that Jesus is with us. We feel inside ourselves the "gentle pull of the Spirit"[19] and, over time, in prayer and patience, in dialogue with others, we reach a solution and a proposal for action.

ACT

The final step, then, following on from our information (seeing) and analysis and theological reflection (discerning), is what action needs to be taken to change the situation, to promote justice and peace, to address the root causes? Our key questions for this stage are:

How would we transform the structures and relationships that produce this situation?

How can we act to empower those who are disadvantaged in this situation?

Who is already working for the good, with whom we can collaborate?

What tactics can we employ to bring about real change?

What resources do we need to employ or procure for this to happen?

One of the questions that Catholic communities might not be used to asking is: *how do we actually bring about change?* So much of the focus of Christian action has been on charity that we are only really beginning to consider what it means to "do justice" (Micah 6:8). In Part III there is a table of **Advocacy Models** that might help to begin the conversation about how to bring about justice. Those who have designed or who benefit from unjust systems are not likely to agree easily to change them. In some political movements, the answer to gaining power from those who will not give it up is to seize it with violence. This is not the Christian way. As we see in the Gospels, there is no violence in Jesus, no violence in God. When Jesus overturned the tables in the Temple, he did not harm people, but interrupted their corrupt practices. Those who benefit from corruption will not become more just if we ask them nicely. There has to be pressure, influence, persuasion, but not violence. Catholic Social Teaching supports strike action, for example, when all reasonable avenues of dialogue have failed. Many Christians have practised civil disobedience in the face of unjust laws. In America, Martin Luther King Jr. was a great witness to the power of the non-violent struggle for justice. In the recommended reading list in Part III, you'll find a reference to *A Gift of Love*, a collection of his inspirational sermons.

One movement that has been successful in bringing about change for the better in recent years is broad-based community organising. Community organising is not a Catholic movement, although many Catholics have been involved, right from the movement's beginning in 1930s Chicago. Austen Ivereigh, in *Faithful Citizens: a practical guide to Catholic Social Teaching and Community Organising*, provides a very helpful survey of community organising and its crossover with CST. Ivereigh quotes at length from a speech by Barack Obama, who worked as a community organiser in a poor area of Chicago. He says that the basic premise of organising is that the problems facing poor communities do not result from a lack of solutions, "but from a lack of power to implement those solutions".[20] The only way for communities to build long-term power is to organise people around a common vision, with local leadership. This means bringing together local groups – those "intermediary bodies" encouraged by subsidiarity – and draw up plans for improvement across a range of issues. Once such a group is formed, local politicians and decision makers will be more responsive to the needs of the community. It also helps to build solidarity in the community – another key CST principle – and break down crippling isolation. In this country, community organising has achieved some real benefits for people, such as the London Living Wage, a result of the campaign by TELCO, The East London Chapter of Citizens.

Catholic communities in America have a longer tradition of working with other groups to bring about change, with community organising as one example. In Britain, this is less the case, perhaps owing to the minority position of the Catholic population and a history of persecution and discrimination. That is changing now and there are opportunities for Catholic communities to work with other groups who are seeking social justice, albeit from a different starting point. Whether the group in question is sufficiently aligned with Catholic and Gospel values is a matter for discernment. As we said in Chapter One, the Holy Spirit is at work in all people of goodwill, prompting them towards the good of humankind. Pope Paul VI said that hope springs from the fact that other people are at work "to undertake actions of justice and peace working for the same ends. For beneath an outward appearance of indifference, in the heart of every man and woman there is a will to live in brotherhood and a thirst for justice and peace, which is to be expanded."[21]

A note on virtue

As we come to the end of this introduction to Catholic Social Teaching, a note on virtues, which have come to the fore again in recent years, especially in our schools. This old-fashioned-sounding concept is undergoing a welcome revival and in fact is at the heart of Catholic Social Teaching. The See-Judge-Act methodology we have been looking at in this chapter is no less than **prudence**, the first of the cardinal virtues. Prudence is described in the *Catechism* as "the virtue that disposes practical reason to discern our true good in every circumstance and to choose the right means of achieving it".[22] This is just what we have been describing. See-Judge-Act has deep roots in Catholic thinking, going back to St Thomas Aquinas, who drew on scripture and the work of Aristotle.

The aim of prudence is to achieve **justice** in the world, our next cardinal virtue. Justice, as we've mentioned before, is the constant and firm disposition to give to God and our neighbour what they are due. Justice towards our neighbour disposes us "to respect the rights of each and to establish in human relationships the harmony that promotes equity with regards to persons and the common good".[23] The pursuit of justice is enabled by our final two cardinal virtues, **courage and temperance**. Courage is the disposition to be constant in our pursuit of the good, even in the face of opposition or persecution. Our role model of courage is Jesus, as we saw in the example of the cleansing of the Temple. Courage means overcoming fear and anxiety; it might even mean making sacrifices for the good. Courage is sustained by our faith in God, as it says in St John's Gospel: "In the world you face persecution. But take courage; I have conquered the world!" (John 16:33). Temperance, which back in the day meant giving up alcohol (which might still be an example of temperance), can be understood more widely as the virtue that "moderates the attraction of pleasures and provides balance in the use of created goods".[24] In other words, it is the kind of lifestyle we were looking at in Chapters Four and Eight, a divestment of possessions so that the goods of the earth may be shared equally. Living simply, so that others might simply live. Drawing on the insights of psychology, there's also a dimension of temperance as self-regulation: as far as we are able not allowing temper or anxiety to mist up our discernment of the good we are called to do.

All of these cardinal, or moral, virtues, can be acquired by human effort and education. That is why it is so encouraging to see our schools increasingly focus on virtue education. While our Gospel values of compassion, justice, truth and freedom might be considered as "held" by the community as the reference points for building the kingdom of God, the cardinal virtues are held by the person and develop in the human heart. They are what we repeatedly do and get better at over time. We develop our *virtue-muscles*, like any other muscles, with a commitment to learning and practice.

These virtues are animated by what we call the theological virtues: **faith, hope and love**. These virtues are "infused by God into the souls of his faithful to make them capable of acting as his children..." (*CCC*, 1813).[25] These virtues are the pledge and presence of the Holy Spirit, breathed into the disciples in the upper room, in the faculties of the human being. Faith is a kind of gateway disposition, the gift of God to be open to his good news. Hope allows us to place our trust in God and not our own efforts. The greatest of all the virtues, the new commandment of Jesus, animating and inspiring all the other virtues, is love. This is the source and goal of our Christian practice, the heart and soul of Catholic Social Teaching, the purpose of all our work: to build the kingdom of God, the civilisation of love.

Questions for individual reflection or group discussion:

The questions for the See-Judge-Act process are all above. What might be worth considering is what needs to happen in our community to engage in the process itself. What are the cultural barriers that might get in the way? Where might you begin: with a small group of the willing and then work outwards from there?

Quotations from sacred scripture and the teaching of the Church:

"And what does the LORD require of you but to do justice, and to love kindness, and to walk humbly with your God?"

Micah 6:8

"Beloved, let us love one another, because love is from God; everyone who loves is born of God and knows God. Whoever does not love does not know God, for God is love. God's love was revealed among us in this way: God sent his only Son into the world so that we might live through him."

1 John 4:7-9

"Impelled by its belief that it is being led by the Spirit of the Lord who fills the whole earth, God's people work to discern the true signs of God's presence and purpose in the events, needs and desires which it shares with the rest of modern humanity. It is faith which shows everything in a new light and clarifies God's purpose in his complete calling of the human race, thus pointing the mind towards solutions which are fully human."

Gaudium et Spes[26]

"In remaining faithful to the gospel and discharging its mission in the world, the church, whose role it is to encourage and enhance whatever truth or goodness or beauty is to be found in the human community, strengthens peace within the human race to the glory of God."

Gaudium et Spes[27]

"Lay people must consider it their task to improve the temporal order. While the hierarchy has the role of teaching and authoritatively interpreting the moral laws and precepts that apply in this matter, the laity have the duty of using their own initiative and taking action in this area – without waiting passively for directives and precepts from others. They must try to infuse a Christian spirit into people's mental outlook and daily behaviour, into the laws and structures of the civil community. Changes must be made; present conditions must be improved. And the transformations must be permeated with the spirit of the Gospel."

Paul VI[28]

"It is not enough to recall principles, state intentions, point to crying injustice and utter prophetic denunciations; these words will lack real weight unless they are accompanied for each individual by a livelier awareness of personal responsibility and by effective action. It is too easy to throw back on others responsibility for injustice, if at the same time one does not realize how each one shares in it personally, and how personal conversion is needed first. This basic humility will rid action of all inflexibility and sectarianism, it will also avoid discouragement in the face of a task which seems limitless in size. The Christian's hope comes primarily from the fact that he knows that the Lord is working with us in the world, continuing in his Body which is the Church – and, through the Church, in the whole of mankind – the Redemption which was accomplished on the Cross and which burst forth in victory on the morning of the Resurrection. This hope springs also from the fact that the Christian knows that other men are at work, to undertake actions of justice and peace working for the same ends. For beneath an outward appearance of indifference, in the heart of every man there is a will to live in brotherhood and a thirst for justice and peace, which is to be expanded."

Paul VI[29]

"We need economies that give to all access to the fruits of creation, to the basic needs of life: to land, lodging and labour. We need a politics that can integrate and dialogue with the poor, the excluded, and the vulnerable, that gives people a say in the decisions that impact their lives. We need to slow down, take stock, and design better ways of living together on this earth."

Pope Francis[30]

"Since it is motivated by the Christian ideal, the Catholic school is particularly sensitive to the call from every part of the world for a more just society, and it tries to make its own contribution towards it. It does not stop at the courageous teaching of the demands of justice even in the face of local opposition, but tries to put these demands into practice in its own community in the daily life of the school."

Congregation for Catholic Education[31]

"The Catholic teacher, therefore, cannot be content simply to present Christian values as a set of abstract objectives to be admired, even if this be done positively and with imagination; they must be presented as values which generate human attitudes, and these attitudes must be encouraged in the students. Examples of such attitudes would be these: a freedom which includes respect for others; conscientious responsibility; a sincere and constant search for truth; a calm and peaceful critical spirit; a spirit of solidarity with and service toward all other persons; a sensitivity for justice; a special awareness of being called to be positive agents of change in a society that is undergoing continuous transformation."

Congregation for Catholic Education[32]

"In Krakow, at the opening of the last World Youth Day, I asked you several times: 'Can we change things?' And you shouted: 'yes!' That shout came from your young and youthful hearts, which do not tolerate injustice and cannot bow to a 'throw-away culture' nor give in to the globalization of indifference. Listen to the cry arising from your inner selves! Even when you feel, like the prophet Jeremiah, the inexperience of youth, God encourages you to go where He sends you: 'Do not be afraid... because I am with you to deliver you' (*Jer* 1:8)."

Pope Francis[33]

References

1. Pope John XXIII, *Mater et Magistra*, 236.
2. Second Vatican Council, *Gaudium et Spes*, 76.
3. Pope Paul VI, *Populorum Progressio*, 81.
4. *Populorum Progressio*, 81.
5. *Populorum Progressio*, 81.
6. Catholic Bishops' Conference of England and Wales, *The Common Good and the Catholic Church's Social Teaching*, 41.
7. Pope Paul VI, *Octogesima Adveniens*, 48.
8. C. Otto Scharmer, *The Essentials of Theory U: core principles and applications* (Oakland: Berrett-Koehler Publishers, 2018), 5.
9. *The Essentials of Theory U*, 5.
10. *The Essentials of Theory U*, 5.
11. *The Essentials of Theory U*, 6.
12. *The Essentials of Theory U*, 6.
13. Pope Benedict XVI, *Deus Caritas Est* ("On Christian Love"), 31.
14. Pope Francis, *Let Us Dream: the path to a better future* (London: Simon & Schuster, 2020), 51.
15. *Let Us Dream*, 52.
16. *Let Us Dream*, 56.
17. *Let Us Dream*, 61.
18. *Let Us Dream*, 61.
19. *Let Us Dream*, 21.
20. Austen Ivereigh, *Faithful Citizens: a practical guide to Catholic Social Teaching and Community Organising* (London: Darton, Longman and Todd, 2010), 32.
21. *Octogesima Adveniens*, 48.
22. *Catechism of the Catholic Church*, 1806.
23. *CCC*, 1807.
24. *CCC*, 1809.
25. *CCC*, 1813.
26. *Gaudium et Spes*, 11
27. *Gaudium et Spes*, 76.
28. *Populorum Progressio*, 81.
29. *Octogesima Adveniens*, 48.
30. *Let Us Dream*, 6.
31. Congregation for Catholic Education, *The Catholic School*, 58.
32. Congregation for Catholic Education, *Lay Catholic in Schools: Witnesses to Faith* (1982), 30.
33. Pope Francis, *Letter to Young People*, January 2017, https://www.vatican.va/content/francesco/en/letters/2017/documents/papa-francesco_20170113_lettera-giovani-doc-sinodo.html, accessed 1 April 2023.

PART TWO

CATHOLIC SOCIAL ACTION

"Spot the CST"

CHARITIES

St Vincent's Centre, Leeds, SVP

On a grey day in January, I visited the St Vincent's Centre in Leeds, an unassuming place in a run-down part of town close to a busy main road. The centre is run by the Society of St Vincent de Paul England and Wales, more commonly known as the SVP, one of our oldest and most respected Catholic charities, founded in Britain in 1844. I grew up in a Catholic culture on the west coast of Scotland and one of the abiding memories of my childhood was the men from the SVP, including my dad, collecting money at the back of the church after Sunday Mass. What always appealed to me about the SVP was that it was about practical support for those in need. Today, the SVP continues in that great tradition to "seek and find those in need, providing practical support and fellowship in a spirit of justice, while tackling the causes of poverty".[1] What has developed in their mission, as you can see from the final phrase in their mission statement, is a commitment to advocacy for justice, as well as the work of charity.

When Caroline and Lorna showed me round the centre that day in Leeds, what I saw was a place of compassion, welcome, warmth and friendship. A place of encounter and accompaniment. You'll get a powerful sense of the impact of the centre on the lives of those who work and visit there in a short film on YouTube. The easiest way to find it is to enter **St Vincent's Support Centre – Sharing Stories** in the search box. The film lasts 6 minutes 38 seconds. I was very moved by all the testimonies, but perhaps it was the words of Arnold, a regular visitor, that touched me most:

> On Mondays, I have friendship group; Tuesday and Thursday is Art and Conversation, drawing and colouring... very good. It's just like coming to a family, very nice people. You can't help but love them. Just makes you feel at home. I'd be lost without St Vincent's, I tell you. I wouldn't know what to do with myself. I'd be lost without the place.

What Arnold's words tell us so powerfully is that the most important thing about the centre, apart from the physical services, is the human contact and support. So many people are isolated and alone, depressed, cold, poor. "People are carrying greater burdens at the moment," was how Caroline put it. Places like the St Vincent's Centre in Leeds befriend those who are isolated and walk with them. In the language of CST that we have been using, they help to restore dignity and agency in a spirit of solidarity. They provide opportunities for lonely people to participate in company. On a more practical level, they provide routes into work. They help people who have been housed by the local authority in empty properties to find affordable furniture and clothing. They provide emergency food referrals, debt advice (much in demand) and language classes for refugees and asylum seekers. They've supported refugees who were housed in a local hotel with nothing but the clothes they were wearing and a pair of flip-flops. They were able to provide clothes and arrange for trips out for those who didn't have enough money to get into the city centre.

One of the biggest problems, Caroline told me, is digital poverty and exclusion. Universal Credit, the main state benefit for those who are out of work or unable to work because of a health condition, is entirely online, but not everyone has access to the internet, or the skills to use digital devices. There is a requirement for claimants to fill out a Universal Credit journal online; failure to do so can result in sanctions. In CST terms, this is a structural injustice that excludes and discriminates against some people. This is not a system that considers the common good, the needs of all people, especially the most disadvantaged. The centre in Leeds provides online help and classes for benefit claimants. There is, however, a bigger piece of work to be done, which is to challenge hostile systems like this that exclude vulnerable people. In recent years, the SVP has taken up this advocacy challenge. To find out more about their commitment to charity and justice, visit: https://www.svp.org.uk/social-justice.

Safe in Faith, Caritas Westminster

Safe in Faith is a project of Caritas Westminster, working to support survivors of domestic abuse, sexual violence and exploitation in ways that understand how their faith impacts their experiences. Although it is a Catholic organisation, based on the values of Catholic Social Teaching, they work with people of all different faiths. I spoke to Nikki Dhillon-Keane, a trained therapist and the founder of Safe in Faith. Below is a summary of our conversation.

Domestic abuse, which can be spiritual as well as violent abuse by one partner in a relationship, is an affront to human dignity. Coercive control is intended to subjugate another. The most effective tactics of the perpetrator are similar to the ones used to break prisoners of war (see Biderman's Chart of Coercion). The same tactics are used by domestic abusers to crush the spirit of their victim. Abuse is often thought of as physical, but it can also be psychological, spiritual and economic: for example by preventing someone from working, making them have to account for every penny spent, keeping them isolated from the community. Connectivity is a key element in psychological happiness. Abusers deliberately undermine this in order to isolate and demean their victim. One of Nikki's clients once asked her where God was in all this suffering. She said it was important not to be trite, or give easy answers, but God is at work through those trying to help, to reverse the damage, forming healing relationships with trauma-informed practice.

What unites Catholic Social Teaching and trauma-informed care is person-centred radical love. It's what you see everywhere in Caritas Westminster: in the work with the deaf community, who are very marginalised, meeting them in their language; in the work with the homeless, those living with food insecurity. It's what it looks like to be Catholic. It's about that and prayer, rooted in Trinitarian love and community. It's about the humility you bring to this work, taking off your shoes because you're standing on holy ground when being with somebody. Feelings experienced are the beginning of relationship, which goes beyond *I see you*. It's about feeling safe and connected, the two keys to psychological happiness.

It's important to understand the layers of complexity involved in people's experiences, so an intersectional approach is essential. The experience of a black man is different from that of a black woman, and in turn a black and disabled woman. We need to respond in solidarity, to meet people in all their complexity with love and understanding, not with a paternalistic approach that falls into the trap of being the rescuer. The model is walking with the other, learning from them. Avoid the temptation of acting as if you, the one who is well, are "fixing" the one who is not. Be aware of your own history of trauma; you're a wounded healer. A beautiful metaphor for post-traumatic growth is the Japanese art of Kintsugi, fixing broken ceramics with powdered gold, leaving a gold seam where the cracks were. We're all here as siblings. It's about listening and walking with you.

In terms of the language we have been using, the work of Nikki and her colleagues takes us to the heart of Catholic Social Teaching, which is the restoration of relationships distorted by the effects of sin. Relationships that are abusive, with one person seeking to dominate and demean another, are, as Nikki said, an affront to human dignity, a barrier to human flourishing. Building a kingdom of love, peace and justice involves living with others in loving and supportive relationships. In our schools and parishes, some of the most important work we can do is to support formation and learning in how to grow in healthy relationships that respect the other; which believe that the greatest joy in the relationship is the flourishing of the other. For more information on the inspirational work of Safe in Faith, visit: https://safeinfaith.org.uk/.

PACT (Prison Advice and Care Trust)
Founded in 1898 as the Catholic Prisoners' Aid Society (CPAS) by a prison chaplain in London to provide care for Catholic prisoners and their families, the Prison Advice and Care Trust (PACT), as it is now called, is a unique and pioneering national charity that supports prisoners, people with convictions and their families, inspired by Catholic Social Teaching. Language is all-important. They do not refer to "offenders" but to people with convictions. It's not about categories of people, who can easily be "othered" or even demonised. It's about people, who for various reasons have been convicted of a crime and are in prison. PACT's vision, which is so close to the Gospel teaching that how we treat the hungry, the sick and those in prison is how we encounter Jesus (Matthew 25:31-46), is of a society in which justice is understood as a process of restoration and healing. At the heart of this vision is a criminal justice system in which prison is used sparingly and as a place of learning and rehabilitation, and in which the innate dignity and worth of every human being are valued.

When I met Marie Norbury, PACT's Faith in Action Volunteering Manager, we talked about Just People, roadshows and workshops for parish communities that PACT has developed in association with Together for the Common Good. The workshops provide an introduction to what imprisonment means and its impact on families, and include the voices of lived experience. They offer a space for people to discern what work God is calling them to in their Christian life, holding out the possibility that it might be to volunteer to support those who are caught up in the criminal justice system. The workshops begin and end with prayer and are deeply rooted in scripture. They explore the common good, what we see in our world today: what's good, what's breaking down. A stimulus for discussion is a short film by the late Jonathan Sacks, the former Chief Rabbi. The animated film can be found on YouTube by entering **Rabbi Sacks on the Politics of Hope**. The key idea is that for the last fifty years we have been focused on the market or the state as the means of human fulfilment and have forgotten society, the life we have in common. We have been obsessed with contract and have forgotten the older biblical concept of covenant, which is based on loyalty and trust. We need to rediscover the lost social language of collaboration.

In the workshops, this is the basis for inviting people to consider how they might contribute to the common good by giving freely of their time and talents to reweave the torn fabric of society, beginning with those who are the most marginalised and cut off from participation and human flourishing. This is often those who are in prison, with little opportunity for human contact and rehabilitation, or those who have been released from prison, who are looking to rebuild their lives and be part of a community. The workshop uses scripture to help reflection, especially the Good Samaritan, which we looked at in some detail in Part I, as well as the story of the Good Thief in Luke's Gospel (23:39-43). Participants are invited to discern how they might reach out to the wounded one by the side of the road in their community, perhaps as a prison visitor, or a volunteer at a prison visitor centre.

Those who have gone on to volunteer with PACT have been transformed by the experience. Archie, who attended a Just People workshop and then volunteered at a prison visitor centre, said:

> For me as a practising Catholic, volunteering with PACT has helped me live out Jesus' call to visit prisoners. In serving families and friends of prisoners I have appreciated the privilege and responsibility of showing compassion and mercy to those who are often rejected by society, never to be forgiven. My volunteering role has reinforced in me that I am very fortunate and that others who are made in God's image are suffering every day.

To find out more about the inspirational work of PACT, visit: https://www.prisonadvice.org.uk/.

SCHOOLS

Andy Lewis, St Bonaventure's School, Forest Gate, London

I met up with Andy Lewis, the Deputy Head for Pastoral and Catholic Life at St Bonaventure's School in Forest Gate, in east London. St Bon's, as it is affectionately known, was founded in 1877 by Franciscan Friars and is one of the oldest Catholic boys' schools in the country. Andy told me that Cardinal Manning, who helped to bring the London Docks Strikes to an end in 1889, also helped to divert funds from church building programmes for the setting up of the school. From its very beginning, the school had deep roots in Catholic Social Action, so it's only fitting that they were one of the founding members of TELCO (The East London Citizens Organisation we mentioned in Chapter Ten), and involved in their Living Wage campaign. Andy told me that one of the pupils once said that his mum was dead. This caused great concern among the staff, of course, but it transpired that the boy's mum wasn't dead, but because she had to work multiple shifts to provide for her family, the boy never saw her, so it felt as if she was dead. This story is much cited by Citizens UK as the story that kick started the Living Wage initiative.

Another campaign for the school has been to improve safety on routes to and from school (this made me think of that dangerous road from Jerusalem to Jericho). There has been violence in the area, which has tragically affected the school. Their approach to a solution is inspired by the strategies of broad-based organising, which means working across as many groups as possible, building relations and a common purpose, and then approaching the authorities to look at ways of making the community safer. One practical outcome of this has been the creation of local safe havens in shops and cafés. A sign outside tells a young person that they can come inside if they feel unsafe or vulnerable. The pupils have engaged with local shops and businesses, inviting them to support this initiative. This helps to build relationships and trust, breaking down suspicion and the stereotypes some adults may hold about young people.

The school has its own TELCO group, which is rooted in the principles of CST as well as community organising. There is so much overlap between the two. The pupils receive training that helps them to identify local power structures and learn how democracy works, how to navigate barriers to make their community a safer and healthier place for all. The starting point is to consider the world as it is and work towards the world as it should be, occupying the tension between the two. This has a lot in common with the See-Judge-Act approach we looked at in Chapter Ten. Andy and his colleagues are working on creating time and space in the curriculum to embed this approach. Their vision is to form young men and women (the school's sixth form is co-educational) who will leave the school with virtuous characters, inspired by a vision of a just world, with an understanding of how to develop themselves and the gifts they offer.

Sebastien Chapleau, Citizens UK

It was by a happy coincidence that a few days after I spoke to Andy Lewis, I met up with Sebastien Chapleau, the Assistant Director of Citizens UK. Seb was born and brought up in France, on a suburban Paris council estate, where the different groups never talked to each other and some parents had two or three jobs to make ends meet, not seeing much of their children at the weekends. He remembers feeling that the Church ignored poverty and eventually he stopped going to Mass. This started a number of conversations, which included the parish priest. Seb was invited to Mass one Sunday and, to his surprise, during the Mass the parish priest took the people on a walk around the community, inviting them to "see" with the eyes of faith, and discern what they might do to build a better community. These early experiences shaped Seb's faith-inspired commitment to community organising.

He came to Britain in 2001 and studied for a PhD in English and Politics in Cardiff. His experience of academia was of a lot of talking, as he put it, but in the meantime the world was not getting any better. He trained to become a primary school teacher and got a job in Greenwich, London. There he met and was inspired by Bernadette Farrell, the Catholic liturgist and one of the founders of London Citizens. It was here that Seb learned about building the kingdom of God on earth by empowering the agency of ordinary people, getting them in the driving seat of change. He told me that justice needs to build power; it's not going to be handed to you on a plate. Broad-based organising builds the power of community to advocate for practical solutions to systemic problems.

Seb went on to work for Citizens nationally and kept up his links with education, working with a number of schools, including St Bonaventure's, to bring the approaches of community organising to the problems of local communities: building capacity and solidarity, talking about what people have in common and what they can do together to build the common good. I was very struck by one thing Seb said at the end of our conversation. Saul Alinsky, the founder of community organising in the United States, once said that charity keeps the poor poor. In other words, without a commitment to justice, you're not addressing the root causes of poverty, but in fact helping to perpetuate the problem. Catholic Social Teaching has developed a very similar vision for the progress of society.

Zoe Batten, Plymouth CAST

I was delighted to catch up with Zoe Batten, the CEO of Plymouth CAST, a multi-academy trust (MAT) of thirty-six schools in the Diocese of Plymouth. Full disclosure: I was the CEO of Plymouth CAST before Zoe. I was so pleased after I left that she took up the post and has led the MAT from strength to strength. When I met Zoe to talk about CST in schools, I knew well the schools she was talking to me about, but not much about the inspiring project she had introduced shortly after she started. In a nutshell, what Zoe told me about was an intergenerational project bringing together the young people in the schools, mostly primary age, with the elderly in their community in care homes.

After the first lockdown, there was a lot of attention on the plight of the elderly in care and nursing homes. The mortality rate was very high and the sense of isolation, with no visitors allowed, was acute. As the idea of an intergenerational project developed in Plymouth CAST, Zoe and her staff were keen that face-to-face encounter should be at the heart of everything. Around six schools initially were matched with a local care home and arrangements were made for children to visit, accompanied by a member of staff. There was hesitation to begin with. This was an alien environment for the children. Most of their own grandparents would have been a generation younger than the folk they were visiting. Some of the elderly had dementia, which the staff thought might be a challenge for the children, but they showed a natural understanding of the limits of old age.

As the visits continued and relationships developed, a number of activities got under way, including art work, baking, sewing, talking about life events, even learning to write with fountain pens. The children showed empathy and understanding in explaining things to their elderly friends, who in turn enjoyed telling the children what life was like when they were young. When the care home had to go into lockdown again, the schools were determined not to lose touch. It was arranged for some of the elderly to visit the schools in minibuses, but they couldn't come out, so the children came out to see them and played around them, juggling and dancing for their delighted friends. Later on, as restrictions eased, there was a celebration of the project, with assemblies in school which told all the pupils what had been happening. There was one very touching story about the impact of this project. One elderly man had lost his wife and went into depression, not speaking to anybody, barely eating. He had lost all interest in life. The staff tried everything they could to engage with him, but without success. It was a visit from the children that lifted him, that brought back a spark of life, the glimmer of a smile. The children's natural joy and sense of connection reached their sad friend in ways that the adults could not manage.

When I spoke to Zoe, they were in the process of learning from their experience and hoping to expand the project. When the staff, pupils and elderly people reflected, they used words and phrases like friendship, respect, fun, enhancing and touching lives. It was, said one teacher, Gospel values in action. I don't know if the staff or pupils used the language of Catholic Social Teaching to describe what happened, but that in a sense doesn't matter. They were *living* Catholic Social Teaching, embodying it, walking the talk. They were without a doubt helping the elderly people to know their dignity; they were showing real solidarity with the older generations, intergenerational solidarity. They were living out what Pope Francis calls the "culture of encounter", not just as a one-off event, but as accompaniment over time. They were, in their own place and time, building the common good.

Andrew Gorman, Oaklands Catholic School, Waterlooville, Hampshire

I was looking forward to catching up with Andrew Gorman, who is the Head of Maths at Oaklands Catholic School in Hampshire. One of the biggest challenges that Catholic schools face in the coming years is embedding Catholic Social Teaching in the curriculum. This work is under way, but my sense is that it's only just beginning. I've heard some people comment that it works fine in RE and the humanities subjects, but what about maths and science? Fair question. It takes more than a few posters of

Catholic scientists and mathematicians in the classroom. If you can embed CST in maths, I thought, you can embed it anywhere in the curriculum. A few conversations later, I'd been put in touch with Andrew, a Head of Maths who has a passion for CST and for Catholic education. He has managed to combine them in his work. We want to develop great people and great mathematicians, he told me. We want to get the person right first – young people of resilience, compassion and justice – in the belief that the student of maths will follow. He believes that CST has enlivened his maths lessons and it may be no coincidence that his results are way above the national average.

Andrew's approach is simple and effective. When he asks the students to engage in maths work, he gives them a related question about Catholic Social Teaching to go with it. For example, before the class start work on prime numbers, Andrew tells them that the police can use prime numbers to decrypt WhatsApp messages. This can help them to intercept messages between criminal gangs, but it could also be viewed as an intrusion into privacy. What's best for the common good? When it's time for feedback, the students talk about their learning in prime numbers, but also CST. He gave me lots more examples linking quadratic graphs and the distribution of wealth, place value, large numbers and the elimination of debt in the global south, the annual percentage rate and payday loan borrowing by people on zero-hours contracts or benefits that don't cover their basic needs. For Andrew, the CST dimension is an advantage in his lessons. He says it brings maths alive and makes it relevant to the social justice issues of today.

The school is working on expanding Andrew's approach across the curriculum. They have adopted the eight principles of Catholic Social Teaching used by the Oscar Romero Award (see CPD and Further Study in Part III). These principles are referred to at staff briefings and are visible throughout the school, in every classroom.

They have a visual icon for each principle. Every department has a CST champion. I really like that idea; that's the way to develop and embed ideas and practice across a school. Leadership is vital, of course. I was struck by what Andrew's headteacher told him when he joined the school. We're a Catholic school, he said; that means we have a preferential option for the poor. Please make that your mission. I was so impressed by such a clear articulation of the mission of the Catholic school by Andrew's headteacher. So was Andrew. It gave him "permission" to develop his work on embedding CST in the curriculum.

George White, St Paul's Catholic School, Leicester
George White is a transgender man and a Catholic RE teacher, Inclusion Lead at St Paul's Catholic School in Leicester, where he was also a pupil. I'd met George a few times, but I was keen to catch up with him to hear from him on inclusion in Catholic schools. In my own experience as a secondary headteacher (2002–2016), I had encountered a number of young people who identified as gay and a small number who wanted to transition from one gender to another. It was not always easy to know how to deal with such complex pastoral situations, but we do have a clear steer from the *Catechism* when it says that homosexual people "must be accepted with respect, compassion and sensitivity. Every sign of unjust discrimination in their regard should be avoided" (*CCC*, 2358).

George's starting point, when we spoke, was human dignity. That for him is the foundation and, as we've seen already, is the basis of Catholic Social Teaching, inspired by the Gospel. Our conversation very quickly moved on to another key idea for George that he brings to his work in school, namely intersectionality, which considers the complex webs of identity and identification rather than one category to describe and limit the person. George believes that this leads to greater participation. In his school, he runs an

Equality and Diversity Group, which creates a space for dialogue and encounter. In recent years, there have been significant social movements prompted by injustice, for example Black Lives Matter and #metoo. These movements have thrown a necessary spotlight on violent and abusive behaviour against different ethnic groups and women, and have made the case for structural change to combat discrimination.

In school, George resisted the idea of having a Black Lives Matter group, because *all* lives matter. Such groups can be separating, not conducive to the common good. We need to learn from each other and the layered vulnerabilities we experience. An intersectional approach begins with the key questions of justice and human flourishing that apply across all categories of identity: where is there not dignity? Why not? Where is the power? Whose voices are heard; whose voices are muted? What can we do together to challenge and change social structures to make them more inclusive and respectful of the human person? This approach seems to me much more in line with Catholic Social Teaching on the common good, which, as we saw in Chapter Nine, "stems from the dignity, unity and equality of all people" (*Compendium*, 164).

Jen Colley and James Conwell, St Patrick's Catholic Primary School, Thornaby, Stockton-on-Tees

Before I met Jen and James from St Patrick's, I had a look at the school's website and was very impressed by their mission statement:

> Our vision is for St Patrick's to be a place of joy, justice and peace, where everyone is welcomed, loved and forgiven. We will be a school where we learn and grow, following in the footsteps of Jesus. At St Patrick's, our mission is to help build and be the Kingdom of God. We believe that the Kingdom is all around us and grows in each and every person. To build God's Kingdom, we bring joy, justice and peace to our world.

We all know that mission statements can sometimes seem like just a well-intentioned, inspiring declaration on the website or in reception that nobody pays much attention to. In this case, having read the school's reports and spoken to Jen and James, it's clear that the mission statement is a reflection of the lived reality of the school. They walk their talk. What I liked about it so much was the emphasis on core Gospel values, which are at the heart of Catholic Social Teaching: love, justice, peace. Some mission statements seem to be more like adverts for trainers or sports drinks: *if you dream it, you can do it* kind of thing. This is much more about performance values than Gospel values. Of course we want our young people to be resilient and to fulfil their potential, but for the sake of building the kingdom of God, not for personal gain.

It is clear that St Patrick's lives and breathes Catholic Social Teaching, but two things struck me in my conversation with Jen and James. One was that every other week in PSHE the children watch Picture News as a stimulus for reading the signs of the times, for asking that question we started with at the beginning: what's going on? What's going on with people? What does the Gospel want to tell us about what's going on? The school has a Mini Vinnies group (see link to SVP England and Wales), which uses See-Think-Act as a key part of its work, so the school is forming experts in CST, young people who are being trained to read the signs of the times and discern what actions will help to make things better.

The school has a relentless focus on its mission statement. One of the key concepts from the leadership gurus is to overcommunicate the message. At the start of every week the school revisits the mission statement and celebrates those pupils who have been kingdom builders in the school. A mission candle, inscribed with "Seek Ye First The Kingdom of God", is lit every Monday in every classroom. They recall the words of St Paul: "the kingdom of God is… righteousness and peace and joy in the Holy Spirit" (Romans 14:17). At St Patrick's, the light of the Gospel burns brightly.

I've had the privilege of speaking to so many teachers and leaders in our schools who are teaching and applying the social doctrine of the Church. **Clare Faulkner**, the headteacher of Saints Peter and Paul in Lichfield, told me that in her school for half the year they do Relationship and Sex Education, but for the other half of the year in that timetable slot they have lessons in Catholic Social Teaching, using *Caritas in Action*, a resource from Salford Diocese. **Jennifer Rowlands**, the Head of RE at Bellerive FCJ Catholic College in Liverpool, told me about their work with the Catholic Association for Racial Justice (CARJ) Merseyside and their Leadership Ambassadors Programme, which aims to train young leaders with a social conscience, inspired by Catholic Social Teaching. **Sam Cantillon**, Chaplain at De La Salle School, St Helens, told me about the work they were doing inspired by their core Lasallian values, which include concern for the poor and social justice. In conjunction with Merseyside Police, they have been running Mentors in Violence Prevention for Year 10 students. MVP is a peer-education programme that provides young people with the language and framework to explore and challenge the attitudes, beliefs and cultural norms that underpin gender-based violence, bullying and other forms of abuse, while building resilience and promoting positive mental health. By supporting schools in taking a "whole-school" approach to early intervention and prevention of bullying, harassment and risky behaviours, the programme empowers pupils to identify and communicate concerns with peers and school staff alike. In the context of the misogyny and the toxic effects of social media that we mentioned in Chapter Six, this programme is a powerful way to form in our young people a commitment to the dignity of the human person and healthy, respectful relationships.

Given the scope of this book – an introduction to Catholic Social Teaching – this can only be a glimpse, some snapshots, of Catholic

Social Action in our schools and charities. It would be very helpful if our academic community could develop some large-scale research projects looking at the understanding, expression and impact of CST, especially in our schools.

Reference

1. St Vincent de Paul Society England and Wales, https://svp.org.uk/about-us, accessed 3 June 2023.

PART THREE

RESOURCES AND SIGNPOSTS

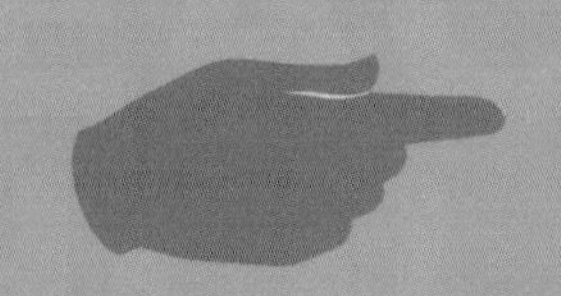

CATHOLIC SOCIAL TEACHING MILESTONES:
Papal Social Encyclicals, Exhortations and Vatican II documents

Rerum Novarum ("On the Condition of Labour"). Pope Leo XIII, 15 May 1891

Quadragesimo Anno ("On Reconstruction of the Social Order"). Pope Pius XI, 15 May 1931

Mater et Magistra ("On Christianity and Social Progress"). Pope John XXIII, 15 May 1961

Pacem in Terris ("On Establishing Universal Peace in Truth, Justice, Charity and Liberty"). Pope John XXIII, 11 April 1963

Gaudium et Spes (Pastoral Constitution on the Church in the Modern World). Vatican II, 7 December 1965

Populorum Progressio ("On the Development of Peoples"). Pope Paul VI, 26 March 1967

Octogesima Adveniens ("On the Eightieth Anniversary of *Rerum Novarum*"). Pope Paul VI, 14 May 1971

Laborem Exercens ("On Human Work"). Pope John Paul II, 14 September 1981

Sollicitudo Rei Socialis ("On Social Concern"). Pope John Paul II, 30 December 1987

Centesimus Annus ("On the Hundredth Anniversary of *Rerum Novarum*"). Pope John Paul II, 1 May 1991

Deus Caritas Est ("On Christian Love"). Pope Benedict XVI, 25 December 2005

Caritas in Veritate ("On Integral Human Development in Charity and Truth"). Pope Benedict XVI, 29 June 2009

Evangelii Gaudium ("The Joy of the Gospel"). Pope Francis, 24 November 2013

Laudato Si' ("On Care for Our Common Home"). Pope Francis, 24 May 2015

Fratelli Tutti ("On Fraternity and Social Friendship"). Pope Francis, 3 October 2020

All of these documents are available on the Vatican's website, www.vatican.va. If you enter any of the titles above into an online search engine, you'll be directed to the document on the Vatican website.

It's also worth remembering that many national bishops' conferences publish their own documents on social teaching. A notable example in England and Wales was published in 1996:

The Common Good and Catholic Social Teaching. Catholic Bishops' Conference of England and Wales, 1996. This is available at: https://www.cbcew.org.uk/documents-and-publications/.

CATHOLIC SOCIAL TEACHING CALENDAR

A good way to integrate CST into the life of your community is to celebrate some of the exemplary witnesses in humanity's long struggle for peace and justice, the key documents, or global observance days. Schools, parishes and charities could use liturgies, assemblies, INSET days, fundraising or advocacy campaigns for formation and education.

The list below is not exhaustive, but offers some of the key milestones from the liturgical calendar as well as UN and other international days. You might want to add your own dates from the charism of your community, or themes of particular resonance for you.

JANUARY

1 January: World Day of Peace. An annual celebration by the Catholic Church, dedicated to universal peace, held on 1 January, the Solemnity of Mary, Mother of God. Pope Paul VI established it in 1967, being inspired by the encyclical *Pacem in Terris* of Pope John XXIII.

15 January: Birthday of Martin Luther King Jr., the de facto leader of the civil rights movement in mid-twentieth-century America. Inspired by his Christian faith, he was a prophetic witness to justice in the face of systemic racial discrimination. https://thekingcenter.org/

18-25 January: Week of Prayer for Christian Unity. Divisions between Christians are still sadly the cause of violence and strife. We pray this week for unity among the followers of Christ. Visit the Churches Together in Britain and Ireland website for resources: https://ctbi.org.uk/.

27 January: Holocaust Memorial Day. We must never forget the horrors inflicted on the Jewish people by the Nazi regime. We commit ourselves anew to stand against anti-Semitism and racial discrimination in all its insidious forms. For resources and information, visit: https://www.hmd.org.uk/.

31 January: Feast of St John Bosco. Better known as Don Bosco, a nineteenth-century Italian who dedicated his life to the street children in northern Italy who were suffering from the effects of industrialisation and urbanisation. He founded the Salesians of Don Bosco.

FEBRUARY

4 February: International Day of Human Fraternity. In 2020, the United Nations declared 4 February as a day to promote and celebrate greater cultural and religious tolerance. For more information, visit: www.un.org/en.

8 February: Feast of St Josephine Bakhita. International Day of Prayer and Awareness Against Human Trafficking. Some 49 million people are in slavery today, more now than ever before. For more information and resources, visit the website of Bakhita House, a project of Caritas Westminster: https://www.caritaswestminster.org.uk/bakhita-house.php.

11 February: Feast of Our Lady of Lourdes, World Day of the Sick. This day was introduced by Pope John Paul II as a reminder to the Catholic community to pray for the sick and their caregivers. It is an opportunity to raise awareness of health services and the extent to which they are accessible by all.

12 February: Red Hand Day, or the International Day against the Use of Child Soldiers. Every year since 2002, this day has raised awareness of the use of child soldiers and urged politicians to commit to ending the use of anybody under the age of eighteen in military organisations.

20 February: World Day for Social Justice. In 2007, the United Nations declared that a day to promote and celebrate social justice globally would be held on this day. For details of the theme for the year, visit the UN website: www.un.org/en.

Friday of First Week in Lent. Lent Fast Day. For resources and suggestions of how to get involved, visit: https://cafod.org.uk/fundraise/family-fast-day.

Three Sundays before 1st Sunday of Lent: Racial Justice Day. For information and resources, visit the website of the Catholic Association for Racial Justice at: https://www.carj.org.uk/.

MARCH

22 March: World Water Day. An annual United Nations observance day since 1993 to celebrate water and raise awareness of the two billion people in the world without access to safe water. See UN website for more details: https://www.un.org/en/observances/water-day.

24 March: Feast of St Oscar Romero, one of the patron saints of Caritas Internationalis and patron saint of Caritas Social Action Network. Oscar Romero, the Archbishop of San Salvador, was assassinated while saying Mass on this day in 1980. He was a prophetic voice for justice and human dignity in El Salvador during the years of the military dictatorship. He embodies the preferential option for the poor. For more information and a bank of resources, visit: http://www.romerotrust.org.uk/.

26 March. Anniversary of the publication in 1967 of ***Populorum Progressio***, by Pope Paul VI. A good day to revisit this groundbreaking document in the school or parish and discuss some of its key passages. Why not try paragraph 21 on truly human conditions, or have a look at the radical vision for the common good in paragraph 24?

APRIL

7 April: Feast of Jean Baptiste de la Salle, patron saint of teachers, founder of all the Lasallian schools worldwide. Lasallian education centres on Catholic values and personal relationships, emphasising academic excellence, faith formation, inclusion, respect for the individual, service and social justice. https://www.lasalleigbm.org/

11 April. Anniversary of the publication in 1963 of ***Pacem in Terris***, by Pope John XXIII. Why not have a look at paragraphs 11-33, which outline the rights and duties of the human person?

MAY

1 May: Feast of St Joseph the Worker. St Joseph has two feast days. On 19 March we celebrate St Joseph, the husband of Mary. On 1 May we celebrate St Joseph the Worker. Joseph, the father of Jesus, was a carpenter. We can only imagine the skills and values Jesus learned working with his father. This is a good day to highlight the dignity of workers.

1 May. Anniversary of the publication in 1991 of ***Centesimus Annus*** by Pope John Paul II. Why not have a look at paragraph 36, which reflects on the important distinction in the consumer age between "having" and "being".

9 May: Birthday of Peter Maurin in 1877, co-founder of the Catholic Worker Movement. Biography can be found here: https://catholicworker.org/pm-biography-html/. Maurin was also known for his **Easy Essays**, his vision of a Christian social order written in short, accessible, free-verse poems. To see some of them, visit: https://catholicworker.org/easy-essays-html/.

15 May. Anniversary of the publication in 1891 of ***Rerum Novarum*** by Pope Leo XIII (why not have a look at paragraph 3 to recall the powerful prophetic voice of this encyclical); in 1931 of ***Quadragesimo Anno*** by Pope Pius XI (why not have a look at paragraph 57 to recall the strong emphasis on social justice in this encyclical); in 1961 of ***Mater et Magistra*** by Pope John XXIII (why not have a look at the short paragraphs from 228-237, which deal with the importance of putting CST theory into practice).

21 May: Feast Day of Blessed Franz Jägerstätter. Born in St Radegund, Austria in 1907. Executed on 9 August 1943 at Brandenburg Prison for his conscientious objection to serving in Hitler's army. On 26 October 2007, Franz was Beatified in his home Diocese of Linz in Austria. For more information on this courageous witness to peace, visit: https://paxchristi.org.uk/resources/peace-people-2/blessed-franz-jagerstatter/.

24 May. Anniversary of the publication in 2015 of ***Laudato Si'*** by Pope Francis. A good day to look again at some key passages in this rich, groundbreaking social encyclical. Why not have a look at paragraphs 222-227 on Joy and Peace and the Christian spirituality of integral ecology?

29 May: Feast day of St Pope Paul VI, the pope who saw the Second Vatican Council to a conclusion and produced some of the key social encyclicals of the twentieth century.

31 May: Feast of the Visitation of the Blessed Virgin Mary. A good day to read St Luke's account (1:39-56) of Mary's visit to her relative Elizabeth, who was also pregnant by a miracle of God. Mary's Song of Praise, the Magnificat, is a prophetic vision of the reversal of the world's values, when the powerful are brought down and the lowly lifted up.

End of May: Laudato Si' Week. Register with the *Laudato Si' Movement* for more information: https://laudatosiweek.org/.

JUNE

Third Sunday in June: Day for Life. A day set aside by the Church to celebrate the dignity and wonder of life from conception to natural death. https://www.dayforlife.org/home/about/

20 June: World Refugee Day. International day organised by the United Nations to celebrate and honour refugees around the world; established in 2001, in recognition of the fiftieth anniversary of the 1951 Convention Relating to the Status of Refugees, of which the UK was a founding signatory.

Refugee Week. Each year around World Refugee Day on 20 June, a UK-wide festival is held to celebrate the contributions, creativity and resilience of refugees and people seeking sanctuary. For more information and how to get involved, visit: https://refugeeweek.org.uk/.

29 June. Anniversary of the publication in 2009 of ***Caritas in Veritate*** by Pope Benedict XVI. So much to reflect on in this long and powerful encyclical, following the financial crash of 2008. Why not have a look at paragraph 45 on the need for a people-centred, ethical economics?

JULY

Second Sunday in July: Sea Sunday. Every year churches around the world celebrate Sea Sunday. It is a day for people to come together to pray for seafarers and those in the fishing industry, and thank them for the vital role they play in all of our lives. For resources and more information, visit the website of Stella Maris at: https://www.stellamaris.org.uk/seasunday/.

15 July: Birthday of Cardinal Manning in 1808. Cardinal Manning was a key figure in the resolution of the London Dock Strike in 1889. Around 130,000 dockers went on strike for more reliable pay and better conditions. Find out more about Cardinal Manning and the London Dock Strike in this article by Jenny Sinclair, the founding director of Together For the Common Good: https://togetherforthecommongood.co.uk/from-jenny-sinclair/to-live-a-decent-life-2.

Fourth Sunday of July: World Day for the Elderly and Grandparents. In 2021, Pope Francis instituted a Church-wide celebration of a World Day for

Grandparents and the Elderly, to be held on the fourth Sunday of July, close to the liturgical memorial of Saints Joachim and Anne, the grandparents of Jesus. This day helps us to remember that the elderly are a gift and we have a duty to ensure that they are looked after well in their final years.

31 July: Feast of St Ignatius of Loyola. Ignatius founded the Jesuit order, which in recent years has been closely associated with the preferential option for the poor. One of their "works", the Jesuit Refugee Service, is dedicated to serving, accompanying and advocating on behalf of refugees. https://www.jrsuk.net/

AUGUST

1 August: Feast of St Alphonsus Mary di Liguori. In the eighteenth century, St Alphonsus founded the Redemptorist Order, with a charism for preaching clearly, with particular solidarity with the poor by promoting their rights to justice and freedom. For more information, see: https://www.redemptorists.co.uk/who-we-are/our-founder-st-alphonsus.html.

14 August: Feast Day of St Maximilian Kolbe, a Polish Franciscan friar who spoke out against the Nazi regime, was arrested and sent to Auschwitz concentration camp. In an act of ultimate solidarity, he offered to take the place of one of the ten men (who was married with a child) who had been selected to die by starvation in retribution for the escape of some prisoners. He led the condemned men in their starvation cell in prayers until the end.

SEPTEMBER

14 September. Anniversary of the publication in 1981 of ***Laborem Exercens*** by Pope John Paul II. Why not have a look at the end of section 15 and the proposals that workers should have more ownership of their workplace?

1 September: World Day of Prayer for the Care of Creation and the beginning of the **Season of Creation**, which ends on **4 October** (see **Feast of St Francis of Assisi**). For more information and inspiration, visit the *Laudato Si' Movement* website: https://laudatosimovement.org/news/what-is-the-season-of-creation/.

5 September: Feast of Saint Mother Teresa of Calcutta, one of the patron saints of Caritas Internationalis. Born in Albania in 1910, Mother Teresa founded the religious order the Missionaries of Charity, which serves the poorest of the poor all over the world.

Second Sunday in September: Education Day. An ecumenical event to celebrate education, which has been marked for over one hundred years in England and Wales. Each year there will be a different theme. For more details, visit: https://www.catholiceducation.org.uk/schools/education-sunday.

Third Sunday in September: Evangelii Gaudium Day. Pope Francis calls on the Church to embark on a fundamental change of direction when it comes to evangelisation, no longer relying on past structures and actions but to read the signs of the times and act passionately in proclaiming the unique message of the Gospel that brings joy to all people who receive it with an open heart. A good day to read *Evangelii Gaudium*, issued by Pope Francis in 2013.

27 September: Feast of St Vincent de Paul. Born in 1581 in Gascony, Vincent studied for the priesthood and was ordained in 1600. In 1617, two events changed his life. After hearing the confession of a dying man, he resolved to preach the Good News of Christ's promised redemption, and later that year after appealing for help for a poor sick family he saw many local people bringing them aid. This inspired him to found the Ladies of Charity (AIC), who were devoted to person-to-person help. Many other Vincentian organisations followed. St Vincent died in 1660 and was canonised in 1737. For more information on his life and legacy, visit: https://www.svp.org.uk/our-history.

Last Sunday in September: World Day of Migrants and Refugees. The Church has been celebrating the World Day of Migrants and Refugees (WDMR) since 1914. It is always an occasion for expressing concern for different vulnerable people on the move; to pray for them as they face many challenges; and to increase awareness about the opportunities that migration offers.

OCTOBER

3 October. Anniversary of the publication in 2020 of ***Fratelli Tutti*** by Pope Francis. A good day to revisit some of the key messages of this encyclical, perhaps in school assemblies or collective worship. There is so much to reflect on in this rich and inspiring encyclical, but why not have a look at paragraphs 215-221 on a new culture of dialogue and encounter?

4 October: Feast of St Francis of Assisi, the patron saint of ecology, described by Pope Francis as the example "par excellence of care for the vulnerable and of an integral ecology, lived out joyfully and authentically" (*Laudato Si'*, 10).

11 October: Feast of St Pope John XXIII, who convened Vatican II and published key social encyclicals (see above).

Mid-October: Challenge Poverty Week in England and Wales. For more information, see: https://challengepoverty.co.uk/.

Second Week in October: Prisons Week. For more than forty years, this week has been an invitation to pray for all those affected by prisons, prisoners and their families, victims of crime and their communities. For more information on Catholic charities working in the criminal justice system, visit: https://www.prisonadvice.org.uk/ or http://www.outtherecharity.org/.

22 October: Feast of St Pope John Paul II, who was pope from 1978 until his death in 2005. In that time, he brought the Gospel to some 130 countries on his travels abroad and produced a rich body of teaching, including some of the milestone encyclicals in Catholic Social Teaching.

NOVEMBER

3 November: Feast of St Martin de Porres. St Martin is one of the three patron saints of Caritas Internationalis, along with St Mother Teresa of Calcutta and St Oscar Romero. For more information on all three and on the mission of Caritas, see: https://www.caritas.org/wordpress/wp-content/uploads/2019/04/ServingOutOfLove.pdf.

11 November: Feast of St Martin of Tours, patron saint of chaplains. St Martin is perhaps best known for the story of cutting his military cloak in two to give half to a naked beggar. In a dream that same night, he saw Jesus dressed in the half of his cloak he had cut for the beggar. Jesus said, "Martin has covered me with his garment."

8 November: Birthday of Dorothy Day in 1897 in New York, Catholic social activist and co-founder of the Catholic Worker Movement. For more information, visit: https://catholicworker.org/timeline-of-the-life-of-dorothy-day/.

25 November: International Day for the Elimination of Violence Against Women. This UN day also marks the launch of the UNiTE campaign (Nov 25-Dec 10), an initiative of sixteen days of activism concluding on International Human Rights Day on 10 December. This campaign, led by the UN Secretary-General and UN Women since 2008, aims to prevent and eliminate violence against women and girls around the world, calling for global action to increase awareness, promote advocacy and create opportunities for discussion of challenges and solutions. For more information, visit: https://www.un.org/en/observances/ending-violence-against-women-day.

Thirty-third Sunday in Ordinary Time: World Day for the Poor. See Vatican website for annual message for the day, which is usually published in June. This is an ideal opportunity to convene all the work of social justice in a diocese for mutual support and inspiration.

Thirty-fourth Sunday in Ordinary Time, Christ the King: World Youth Day. Pope Francis moved the celebration of World Youth Day, initiated by Pope John Paul II, from Palm Sunday to the Feast of Christ the King. For more information, see: https://worldyouthday.com/annual-celebration-of-wyd-moved-to-the-feast-of-christ-the-king.

DECEMBER

1 December: World AIDS Day, designated on 1 December every year since 1988, is an international day dedicated to raising awareness of the AIDS pandemic caused by the spread of HIV infection and mourning those who have died of the disease. World AIDS Day is one of the eleven official global public health campaigns marked by the World Health Organization (WHO), https://www.who.int/. For more information on AIDS prevention and support in the UK, visit: https://caps-uk.org/.

7 December. Anniversary of the promulgation by Pope Paul VI in 1965 of ***Gaudium et Spes***, the document of Vatican II which is most concerned with social issues. This is the Magisterium (teaching) of the Church at its highest level (*Compendium*, 96); hence it is the most significant document in Catholic Social Teaching. To recap on its teaching on the social order and the Gospel, why not have a look at paragraph 26?

10 December: Human Rights Day. Anniversary of the proclamation by the United Nations General Assembly on 10 December 1948 of the Universal Declaration of Human Rights (UDHR), the first global declaration of human rights. For the full text, visit: https://www.un.org/en/about-us/universal-declaration-of-human-rights.

25 December: The Nativity of the Lord. The ultimate act of God's solidarity with the human race. "And the Word became flesh and lived among us" (John 1:14).

25 December. Anniversary of the publication in 2005 of ***Deus Caritas Est*** by Pope Benedict XVI. Why not have a look at paragraph 31a, which reflects on the importance of the formation of the heart?

30 December. Anniversary of the publication in 1987 of ***Sollicitudo Rei Socialis*** by Pope John Paul II. Why not have a look at paragraphs 38-40 for an extended reflection on solidarity?

FURTHER READING: SOME RECOMMENDATIONS

A Gift of Love, by Martin Luther King Jr. (London: Penguin Classics, 2017)

Catholic Social Thought and Catholic Charities in Britain Today: need and opportunity, by Ben Ryan (London: Theos, 2016)

Cathonomics: how Catholic tradition can create a more just economy, by Tony M. Annett (Washington DC: Georgetown University Press, 2022)

Compendium of the Social Doctrine of the Church, Pontifical Council for Justice and Peace (London: Bloomsbury, 2004)

DOCAT: what to do? (San Francisco: Ignatius Press, 2016)

Faithful Citizens: a practical guide to Catholic Social Teaching and community organising, by Austen Ivereigh (London: Darton, Longman and Todd, 2010)

Just Money: how Catholic Social Teaching can redeem capitalism, by Clifford Longley (London: Theos, 2014)

Let Us Dream: the path to a better future, by Pope Francis (London: Simon and Schuster, 2020)

Love in Action: Catholic Social Teaching for every church, by Simon Cuff (London: SCM Press, 2019)

Nature Praising God: towards a theology of the natural world, by Dermot A. Lane (Dublin: Messenger Publications, 2022)

To Heal the World: catechesis on the pandemic, by Pope Francis (Vatican: Libreria Editrice Vaticana, 2020)

Toward a Politics of Communion: Catholic Social Teaching in dark times, by Anna Rowlands (London: T&T Clark, 2021)

PART THREE

CATHOLIC SOCIAL TEACHING

USEFUL WEBSITES FOR EXAMPLES OF SOCIAL ACTION, ADVOCACY AND INFORMATION

Arise Foundation. Today, at around 49 million people, there are more slaves than ever before. Arise is an anti-slavery NGO. To find out more about their mission to end slavery and human trafficking, visit: https://www.arisefdn.org/.

Caritas diocesan agencies in England and Wales. Almost every diocese in England and Wales now has a Caritas agency, ranging greatly in size and scope. Some are services providers, with considerable funding and employed staff. Some are smaller in size with a focus on animating and co-ordinating the work of social justice in the diocese. All have in common a vision of a society built on the Gospel, founded on truth, built up on justice and animated by love. To find out more about your diocesan Caritas, please visit: https://www.csan.org.uk/member/?member_focus=diocesan-caritas-agency.

Caritas Europa. Features extensive resources, including a *Grassroots Participation Handbook*, which is designed to encourage participation at various levels of communal life. Available here: https://www.caritas.eu/grassroots-participation-handbook/.

Caritas Internationalis has more than 160 members worldwide. A member is a national charitable Catholic organisation or a collective group of them that works with the support of their Church. Caritas Internationalis is made up of seven regions. Members of regions work together on common issues, strengthening each other and contributing to global action. They are Africa, Asia, Europe, Latin America and the Caribbean, the Middle East and North Africa (MONA), North America, and Oceania. CSAN and CAFOD (see below) are both members of Caritas Internationalis. For more information, see: https://www.caritas.org/.

Caritas Social Action Network (**CSAN**) is the agency of the Bishops' Conference dedicated to co-ordinating and animating the fight against poverty and injustice in England and Wales. For more information on the extensive network of Catholic independent charities and dioceses working in the field of Catholic Social Action, visit: https://www.csan.org.uk/member/.

Catholic Agency for Overseas Development (CAFOD). See **CPD and Further Study** for more information on the resources available from CAFOD, the official aid agency of the Catholic Church in England and Wales. For other information and resources, visit: https://cafod.org.uk/.

Catholic Centre for Social Thought and Practice, Durham. Features a number of very helpful essays on *Fratelli Tutti*: https://ccstp.org.uk/.

Christians Against Poverty is a Christian charity whose "anchor value" is being Christ-centred. They work with churches, local communities, staff and volunteers across the country to make a difference to the lives of those living in poverty. For practical guidance and to find out more about their projects, visit: https://capuk.org/.

Church Action on Poverty is a national, ecumenical Christian social justice charity, committed to tackling poverty in the UK. Their website features some very helpful resources and publications, including their *Church on the Margins* report. You will also find very powerful testimonies from the voices of lived experience of poverty: https://www.church-poverty.org.uk/.

Citizens UK. The home of community organising. A people-powered alliance dedicated to challenging injustice and building stronger communities. For more information, visit: https://www.citizensuk.org/.

Jesuit Refugee Service (JRS) is an international Catholic organisation, at work in over fifty countries around the world with a mission to accompany, serve and advocate for the rights of refugees and other forcibly displaced persons. JRS UK has a special ministry to those who find themselves destitute as a consequence of government policies and those detained for the administration of immigration procedures. Visit: https://www.jrsuk.net/.

Joint Public Issues Team (JPIT) is the Baptist Union of Great Britain, the Methodist Church and the United Reformed Church working together for peace and justice. To find out more about their range of issues, advocacy campaigns and resources, visit: https://jpit.uk/.

Joseph Rowntree Foundation. How many people are in poverty in the UK? What is poverty? Are some groups affected more than others? For authoritative data on these important questions, see the JRF report, UK Poverty 2023, which can be found at: https://www.jrf.org.uk/report/uk-poverty-2023.

Journey to 2030. Practical and creative resources for schools and parishes to help build communities where integral ecology becomes a reality: https://journeyto2030.org/.

Laudato Si' Movement aims to inspire and mobilise the Catholic community to care for our common home and achieve climate and ecological justice, in collaboration with all people of goodwill. For a wealth of inspiration, information and resources, including a free ***Laudato Si' Movement Prayer Book***, visit: https://laudatosimovement.org/.

Living Wage Foundation is a campaigning organisation that seeks to persuade employers to pay a real Living Wage, which is based on the cost of living. For more information on the differences between the Minimum Wage, National Living Wage and real Living Wage, visit: https://www.livingwage.org.uk/what-real-living-wage.

Marriage Care offers marriage preparation and relationship counselling. They specialise in helping couples build and sustain strong, fulfilling and healthy relationships, and in providing support in times of relationship difficulty. For more information, see: https://www.marriagecare.org.uk/.

St John of God Hospitaller Services. A charity inspired by the religious order St John of God, which runs a number of services to support victims of human trafficking, adults with physical and learning disabilities, the elderly and the homeless. For the voices of the lived experience of those they support, visit: https://sjog.uk/what.php.

The Charles Plater Trust is an independent charitable organisation that makes grants to a wide range of religious and non-religious organisations, people and groups, supporting leadership, social action and applied research projects across England and Wales. The website contains a wealth of insight on Catholic Social Teaching, at: https://www.plater.org.uk/catholic-social-thought/insights.

Together for the Common Good (T4CG) is a national Christian charity dedicated to the renewal of the civic ecology by bringing covenantal thinking into church and civic life. For a range of stimulating thought pieces and information on events and programmes, including Common Good Schools, visit: https://togetherforthecommongood.co.uk/.

CPD AND FURTHER STUDY

Caritas Social Action Network offers a range of publications and information about social action campaigns. You'll also find inspiration from the fifty-four member charities working on the front line of social injustice in England and Wales. For more information, visit: https://www.csan.org.uk/about-csan/publications/ and https://www.csan.org.uk/member/.

The work of the **Catholic Agency for Overseas Development (CAFOD)** is underpinned by Catholic Social Teaching, particularly the principles of human dignity and solidarity, which are two of CAFOD's values. It provides high-quality, easy-to-use CST educational resources, to enhance both the curriculum and the Catholic Life and Mission of the school. In addition, CAFOD offers accessible and engaging workshops for children and young people on Catholic Social Teaching, as well as teacher training (CPD) that deepens knowledge of CST through practical activities, resources, examples and opportunities to live out CST in school.

Resources: CAFOD has developed a wide range of resources to support children and young people of all ages in learning about, and living out, Catholic Social Teaching. These resources include short animations, for example "CST in 3 minutes"; CST for children pack; interactive games; a set of CST cards; posters and many other activities.

Primary (EYFS, Key Stage 1, Key Stage 2): cafod.org.uk/cstprimary

Key Stage 3: cafod.org.uk/cstsecondary

GCSE: cafod.org.uk/gcse

Sixth Form Core RE: cafod.org.uk/sixthform

School-visitor-led workshops for children and young people: CAFOD has fully trained and DBS-checked education volunteers who run workshops with children and young people. These workshops change termly, and frequently include learning about Catholic Social Teaching, what it is and how we can live it out in our world.

Contact schools@cafod.org.uk to find out what we are currently offering and book a CST workshop for your primary or secondary school.

Primary and Secondary CPD: There is a school-staff-led Introduction to CST programme available on CAFOD's website. This is linked to the Catholic Schools Inspection Framework, and consists of a PowerPoint presentation that includes links to relevant short films, supporting interactive resources for group learning, and facilitators' notes including a full script to accompany the presentation.

CAFOD can run whole-day, half-day or twilight CPD on an introduction to Catholic Social Teaching, or exploring *Laudato Si'* and/or *Fratelli Tutti* in more detail.

Visit CAFOD's website to find a developing suite of online CPD modules for individual members of staff, which will include an introduction to CST and other programmes.

Visit cafod.org.uk/cpd for more details, or contact schools@cafod.org.uk to find out more about CAFOD's current CPD opportunities.

St Mary's University in Twickenham, London, offers an MA, PGDip and PGCert in Catholic Social Teaching, the only complete programme in Catholic Social Teaching taught face to face in the UK and Ireland. For more information, visit: https://www.stmarys.ac.uk/courses/postgraduate/catholic-social-teaching.

Catholic Higher and Further Education in England and Wales. For more information on the range of courses offered by Catholic higher and further education institutions in England and Wales, visit: https://www.catholiceducation.org.uk/about-us/higher-and-further-education.

Anna Rowlands has prepared a nine-part CST course focused on schools educators and those interested in social justice. Each module contains a one- to two-hour deep dive into a CST principle, and includes podcast interviews and audio reflections by key practitioners. The modules run on any tablet, phone or laptop device and can be used by individuals or organisations. For more information, email: anna.rowlands@hardyandbyrd.com.

Raymond Friel, the author of this book, works as a part-time freelance consultant offering INSET for schools and MATs on Catholic Social Teaching, the life and mission of the Catholic school and leadership. He has also led sessions on CST for parishes, dioceses and charities. You can find Raymond on Twitter @friel_raymond or email him at raymond@raymondfriel.com.

The Oscar Romero Award supports and recognises schools that wish to embed Catholic Social Teaching in their governance, curriculum and practice. For more information, visit: https://www.romeroaward.co.uk/.

ADVOCACY MODELS With thanks to the team at Caritas Social Action Network

METHOD	PROS
Public Protest **Demonstration** **Letter-writing Campaign**	- Gives sense of public interest/anger - Gives wide scope of people opportunity to participate
Public Critique **Condemnation** (e.g. open letters, press releases)	- Publicises issues and concerns, clarifies position publicly - Can energise supporters and keep debate alive - Easy to do
Awareness-raising **Education** **Briefing Events**	- Aims to change public narratives by educating the public on a situation (e.g. case studies, personal stories) - Not necessarily critical of government, part of broader campaign for change
Research	- Similar to Awareness-raising but more in-depth - Done well, it is hard to counter – provides academic, comprehensive evidence of why change is required
Direct Political Intervention (speeches, votes, amendments from MPs/Peers, engagement with legislation)	- If successful, can completely change the law and underpinning circumstances
Indirect Political Intervention (consultation responses, briefings)	- If successful, can influence the thinking behind political decisions before they become parliamentary battles
Legal Approaches (judicial review)	- Can force overturning of government decisions

	CONS
	Takes significant energy and organisation Can antagonise decision makers How often does it succeed?
	Can antagonise decision makers Unclear how often it succeeds in winning people over
	Slow process that is often only indirectly linked to change Needs good comms / social media / media links to be effective Very hard to measure and assess success
	Requires expertise Very slow Hard to measure and assess success Needs a comms plan to ensure it doesn't just become dust on a shelf
	Requires close relationships with parliamentarians A government with a large majority means it is difficult to change anything without their support Requires high-level political expertise
	Requires expertise and time High effort for often low reward Crowded field
	Requires legal expertise Victories often temporary Danger of seeming to subvert democratically legitimate decisions Antagonises government

CATHOLIC SOCIAL TEACHING

THE PERMANENT PRINCIPLES

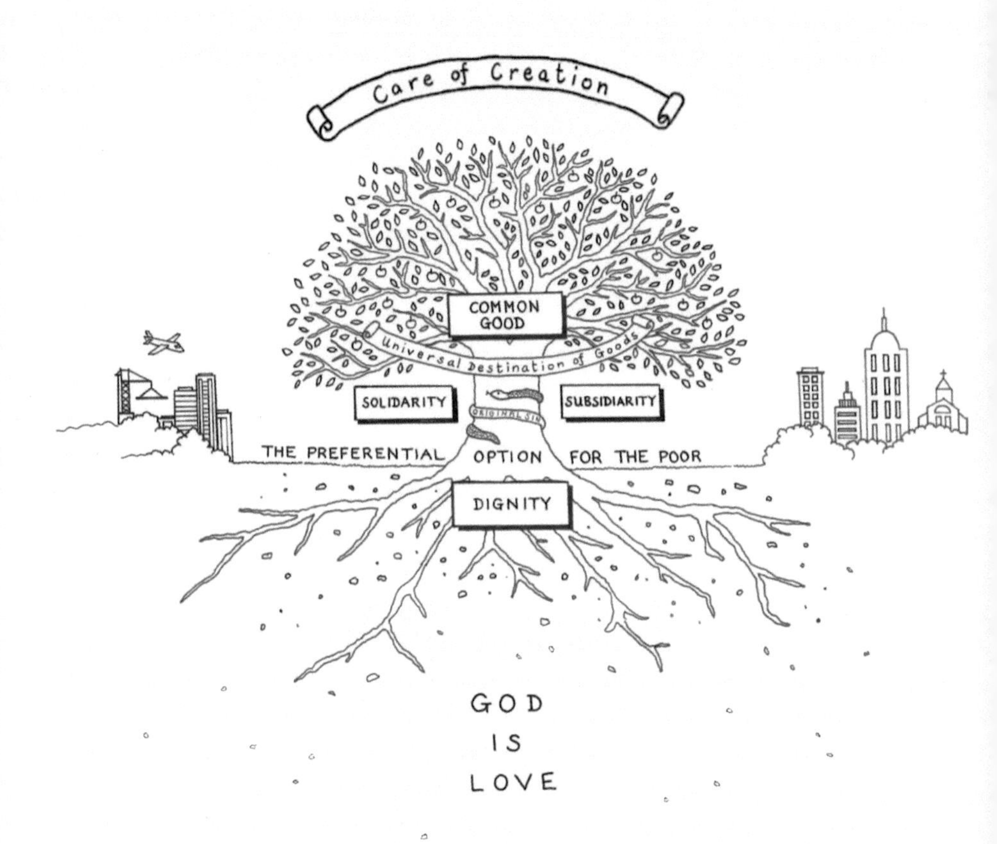

CATHOLIC
SOCIAL
TEACHING